FOODS OF SIERRA LEONE AND OTHER WEST AFRICAN COUNTRIES

A Cookbook
And Food-Related Stories

Rachel C.J. Massaquoi

AuthorHouse™
1663 Liberty Drive
Bloomington, IN 47403
www.authorhouse.com
Phone: 1-800-839-8640

First published by AuthorHouse 4/4/2011

ISBN: 978-1-4490-8154-6 (sc)

Library of Congress Control Number: 2010901111

Food pictures taken by Yeniva Mamie Lucia Massaquoi

Printed in the United States of America

This book is printed on acid-free paper.

authorHOUSE®

Dedication

This book is dedicated to two women who have had a strong positive impact on my family.

It is dedicated to the memory of my mother, Haja Lucia Mamagway Macarthy (Yei). While putting the finishing touches on the book, I suffered a great tragedy – the sudden death of Yei. Her passion for the art of cooking greatly influenced and inspired me to share with you the recipes for the many dishes she had taught me to prepare.

This book also celebrates the life of my mother-in-law, Haja Mamie Massah Massaquoi (Yeamie) for her wonderful support and the contributions she continues to make to the family.

Acknowledgment

My extended family, friends, and acquaintances contributed to this work through discussions, recipe trials, and taste tests. On many occasions, they commented honestly on my dishes and encouraged me to share my cooking knowledge with the world. These contributors motivated me to start and to continue with this work. It is impossible to list them all by name, but my deepest appreciation and thanks go to everyone who helped to make my dream of sharing this vast knowledge about West African foods come true. In particular, I am grateful to my husband Joseph Sr. for his generosity, our daughters Yeniva (who also skillfully took the photographs in this book) and Satta for proofreading this work at different stages, and our son Joseph Jr. and his wife Erika for all their support throughout this project; without each and every one of them, it would have been impossible to complete this work. Last but not the least; I thank Andrew Gillings for the final review and for providing useful editorial suggestions.

Our granddaughter, Luba Halalo Lucia Massaquoi, came into the world exactly 3 months after the death of my mother. Her birth was a great comfort that helped us all to cope with our loss, and made it possible for me to concentrate on finishing this work. I thank Luba, and I thank God almighty for all HIS blessings.

Table of Contents

Introduction

Among my people in West Africa, cooking is an art form we naturally start to learn from a very tender age: first by watching and helping, then by cooking simple meals, and later by preparing more complicated dishes. There are no specific measurements to apply. By the time a child is old enough, she is able to cook any meal merely by sight, smell, and taste. One of my aims in writing this cookbook was to create accurate measurements for the ingredients, while ensuring that the original, traditional, and delectable tastes were maintained. In this regard, I cooked each dish time and time again. After repeated trials, taking into account the specific measurements and flavors required for each dish, I have arrived at what I consider to be those perfect and original West African tastes.

My trials have allowed me to compose more than 100 delectable recipes that are common to Sierra Leone, Liberia, Côte d'Ivoire, Ghana, Togo, Benin, Nigeria, Guinea, the Gambia, and Senegal – written from my perspective as a Sierra Leonean. These meals include rich varieties of vegetable *palaver* sauces, bean sauces, soups and stews, cooked grains, roots, and tubers. *Foods of Sierra Leone and other West African Countries* is a unique cookbook that features a collection of traditional food recipes. However, some 'non-traditional' vegetables, like spinach and collard greens, have been included because of their capacity to take on the taste of traditional vegetables. This factor is important because some traditional vegetables are either disappearing or are not readily available in countries outside the West African region. I, therefore, find the suggested alternatives to be an instructive addition to modern West African cooking. While living in many countries outside of West Africa, I found an absence of ingredients for the traditional dishes I craved; out of necessity, I had to become inventive. I carried out many food trials with alternative vegetables that yielded delicious successes. I have, therefore, incorporated these mouthwatering alternative ingredients in this book so that you may cook these dishes anywhere in the world, at anytime.

A complete West African meal is made up of three components that are served together. The first component is the staple, which consists of carbohydrate-based foods such as rice, yam, or cassava – cooked separately. The second and third components are made up of protein-based foods and vegetables and/or oils; these are always combined and cooked together. Of course, these dishes can be made vegetarian by excluding the meat, fish, and poultry. Nuts are eaten as snacks, but groundnuts (also known outside the region as peanuts) are very popular, both as snacks and as additions to some dishes. Fruits such as mangoes, pineapples, pawpaws, and oranges are sometimes eaten after meals or at any time during the day. Beverages consist mostly of water. Other drinks, prepared from ginger and other plants, are consumed mostly during feasts and celebrations.

The recipes in this book are arranged to show that West African meals start with the main dish. Our meals do not traditionally come with appetizers or starters as a prelude to the main meal.

Nor do they come with desserts, although fresh tropical fruits are often eaten after meals. We, therefore, start directly with the main meal. However, for those who would like these additions to their meals, there are recipes for snacks (see the *Snacks and Accompaniments* chapter) that can be substituted as appetizers or desserts. There are also vegetarian variations of soups and mixed sauces that are included in the *Main Dishes: Vegetarian Soups and Sauces* chapter.

A large selection of ingredients, including palm oil, beef, fish, beans, fresh green vegetables, rice, yams, plantains, cassava, *fufu*, groundnuts, and pepper, are available in and around the food market stalls in West Africa. Most of these ingredients are also readily available in Asian and other ethnic food stores outside the region. Therefore, it is possible to cook all of the dishes in this cookbook no matter where you are in the world.

Some foods: Bottom, Beans Akara and pepper sauce, above from left, fresh fish palm oil soup and check rice, regular stew, fried fish and joloff rice in the background.

Food Categories

This chapter presents some of the frequently used ingredients that make up the foods of Sierra Leone and other West African countries. The food categories are comprised of carbohydrates (staples), proteins, vegetables, and tropical fruits as well as oils, nuts, and seeds. Variations of herbs and spices are also added to some dishes.

CARBOHYDRATES (STAPLES): This category consists of grains, tubers, and tree crops. Grains include rice, sorghum, and millet; tubers include yam, cassava, and sweet potato; and tree crops include plantain, breadfruit, and green banana. These foods are prepared by a boiling, frying, or roasting method. They are served alongside a soup, stew, or mixed sauce.

Rice and other Grains: Rice is extensively eaten in most of the countries in the region and is a staple in Sierra Leone and Liberia. Over the years, rice consumption has increased in popularity in some parts of Guinea, Ghana, Nigeria, Côte d'Ivoire, Togo, Gambia, Senegal, and Benin. There are several varieties of African rice – some grown in the inland valley swamps, some in the mangrove and associated swamps, and still others in the highlands. There are long, medium, and short grains, most of which are white in color. However, there is a unique variety, with a pinkish-brown color, that grows in the highlands of Sierra Leone and is believed to be very rich in vitamin B. African rice, unfortunately, is grown only at a subsistence level. Therefore, the only rice that is available to the majority of the population in West Africa is imported from Asia and North America.

Long, slender grains tend to be highly popular and go very well with a variety of soups, stews, and mixed sauces. Parboiled rice goes very well with slippery sauces. Medium and short grains go very well with soups and stews. Nevertheless, all types of grains can be eaten with soups, stews, and mixed sauces, according to preference and availability.

Millet, sorghum, and couscous are the other mainstays of the West African diet and are typically served with soups and stews. Millet and sorghum prosper in areas that are affected by drought. In West Africa, these grains are popularly grown and eaten in countries such as Burkina Faso, Niger, and parts of Nigeria. Though couscous has its origins in North Africa, it has become quite popular in grain form in West Africa, particularly in parts of Senegal, Mali, Niger, and Nigeria.

Cassava, other Tubers, and Tree Plants: The cassava plant is a woody shrub that is easy to grow. Once planted, it requires very little attention. The plant, which has the capacity to kill weeds while leaving the cassava plant healthy, often sheds old leaves as new ones grow. The old leaves then serve as adequate manure. In the region, when we say cassava, we mean the cassava tuber, and we refer to the leaves as cassava leaf. The leaves, which are rich in proteins, vitamins, and minerals, are eaten as a vegetable. Cassava tubers are a major source of carbohydrate. The mature cassava tuber can be preserved underground for several months. Cassava grows year-round and is available in all seasons, whether dry, rainy, hot, or cold. In the deep south of Sierra Leone, where fish are in abundance, people eat more cassava with fish than they do with rice. Due to its year-round supply, cassava is useful between the periods of plentiful food and scarce food. It is therefore very versatile. Cassava can be cut in large, medium, small, or even miniscule sizes. These pieces can be boiled and served with soups, stews, or beans. An alternate method of preparation is to grate and ferment cassava in order to cook *fufu*. *Fufu* is then served with certain types of soups and mixed vegetable sauces. Processed cassava also produces *gari* also known as *farina*, which is a form of textured flour that is widely eaten in West Africa. In Côte d'Ivoire, cassava tubers are processed into a couscous-like grain known as *Attieke*. It is a staple starch in that country and is also eaten in other countries in the region.

Other tubers, such as yam, cocoyam, and sweet potato, are also eaten. Yam is a staple in some parts of Nigeria and Ghana. Normally, it is boiled and served with stews, soups, or fried fish, together with steamed vegetables. Additionally, it can be eaten as a snack. Sweet potato can also be fried and roasted.

Tree crops, such as plantain and breadfruit, can be boiled, fried, or roasted. Like sweet potato, the fried and roasted plantain and breadfruit can be served by itself to be eaten as a snack. Corn is often boiled, roasted, or fermented and cooked as a type of *fufu*. Roasted and boiled corn is often eaten as a snack.

PROTEIN: Meat, game meat and poultry, broad beans, fish, and shellfish are some of the food items in this group. Note that although broad beans may be considered as a vegetable in other cultures, it is treated as a protein item in some areas across the region. This is understandable considering its high protein content and also because it is cheap and more available than other protein items.

Meats: The main meat sources are beef, goat, sheep, and pork.

Game Meat and Poultry: Game meat, commonly referred to as "bush meat," such as deer are eaten throughout West Africa. Domesticated fowls, game fowls, and other kinds of meat are also consumed. The domesticated fowl, much like the game fowl, runs wild and feeds on natural foods. However, the domesticated fowl is a healthier and more affordable option for most people. As these birds have lean and very hard bodies, they need a longer time to cook. But, in the end, they yield a delicious flavor.

Likewise, broiler chickens, domesticated fowls, and game fowls are the types of poultry that are eaten throughout the region. Broiler chickens are softer, take less time to cook, and work better when cooked in soups and stews.

Fish and other Seafood: Shellfish and fish, from the sea, lakes, and rivers, also form part of the protein diet. Smoked fish is easier to preserve and is used in most mixed sauces. Shellfish, like shrimp, is either cooked in its fresh state or smoked.

VEGETABLES: There are several varieties of traditional West African vegetables. Sadly, due to mass urbanization and lack of adequate research that documents these crops; many of these vegetables remain unknown to the outside world. Though some are even disappearing, there are thankfully many more that are still available. In addition, there are other vegetables outside the region that are similar in taste to some of these endangered vegetables. For example, Italian spinach smells very much like traditional potato leaves, and when cooked using the traditional potato leaf recipes (see the *(Mixed Sauces 1) Cassava Leaves, Potato Leaves, and Others* chapter), it can taste just like potato leaf sauce. I have, therefore, included recipes for some of the vegetables that can be used as a substitute for traditional vegetables.

'Slippery' Vegetables: These vegetables, such as okra, okra leaves, and *crain-crain,* have a naturally smoother consistency when cooked. In the absence of *crain-crain*, Italian spinach and okra can be combined to produce a taste similar to *crain-crain.* (See the *crain-crain* recipe in the *(Mixed Sauces 3) Okra, Crain-Crain, Baby Spinach, Beans, and Others* chapter).

Green Leafy Vegetables and Flowers: These include cassava leaves, potato leaves, bitter leaves, sorrel leaves, sorrel flowers, greens, *cocoyam* leaves, and pumpkin leaves. Cassava leaves are the leaves of the cassava tuber. Potato leaves are from a family of sweet potatoes that yield only leaves and very little or no tubers. The other leaves are mostly the leaves of a tuber.

Pods: These vegetables include *tola* and *bor-boueh* which are wild mango seeds. While mostly available in the West African region, some Asian and other ethnic food stores, outside the region, also carry them.

Buds: These include a wide variety of garden eggs and eggplants. Garden eggs, a useful yet forgotten health food, are believed to contain a very large proportion of fiber; when used in a diet, bowel movements will remain regular.

Some garden eggs are shaped like traditional eggs, some are oblong, and others resemble round tomatoes. They are either striped or unstriped, and their colors range from white, cream, yellow, and navy blue to green (when unripe) and red (when ripe). Their taste varies from bland to sweet and bitter to slightly bitter. Garden eggs can be used when preparing potato leaves, mixed sauces, okra sauces, and vegetables steamed over cooking rice. The latter dish, called *pemahuin* in Sierra Leone, is a combination of rice and potato leaves where the potato leaves are steamed over cooking rice.

Another kind of garden egg grows in Sierra Leone on a plant called the *pillaah*. The plant produces flowers that develop and grow into this special garden egg. The leaves remain fresh, and both the leaves and the garden egg are edible. This special garden egg is usually green, yellow, white, or cream in color and its shapes is bigger and rounder. It is used in the cooking of cassava leaves, okra leaves, and broad beans mixed sauces. A combination of *pillaah* leaves and its related garden eggs can also be cooked as a vegetable sauce. This type of sauce, however, is rapidly disappearing. Today, mostly older women from eastern and southern Sierra Leone cook it. It is a very nutritious and delicious sauce, and I hope more people will learn to cook it with the help of this book.

Eggplant: A universal vegetable that is well known in many cultures. West Africans use it for cooking stews and cassava leaves.

Dried Vegetables, Beans, and Dried Mushrooms: There is a particular mushroom in Sierra Leone, which looks exactly like the portobello mushroom, that we call *kporway*. It grows in the wild much like many other varieties of edible mushrooms. It is cooked in its fresh state or dried for preservation. Dried mushrooms and other vegetables are very popular in this region. For example, a particular dried mushroom called *kormaphai* was a crown favorite in many Sierra Leonean dishes.

All vegetables must be properly cleaned before cooking. The method of preparation depends on the type of vegetable being cooked. Cassava leaves, for example, have to be ground finely; bitter leaves must be processed to get rid of most of its bitterness; and sorrel leaves need to be boiled, and then kept in cold water for a few hours, and finally, cooked to get rid of its sour taste. All other green leafy vegetables and slippery vegetables may be chopped. Okra can be cooked whole or chopped.

Many years ago, it was common for housewives in rural Sierra Leone to dry and grind garden eggs and okra and separately preserve them for use during seasons when they were not available. Dried okra was sometimes preserved whole to cook as a vegetable. Dried, powdered okra was preserved and used as a food thickener. Because of their flavors, dried, powdered garden eggs were added to potato leaves and *pemahuin* dishes.

TROPICAL FRUITS: There are several varieties of domesticated and wild fruits. Many wild fruits remain unknown, but are available in the rural areas. Among the domesticated fruits are mangoes, pawpaws (also called papaya in other parts of the world), ripe bananas, and pineapples. Likewise, there are a large number of plums and berries to be found in the wild.

OILS, NUTS, AND SEEDS: Nuts and seeds are often used to flavor and thicken sauces, soups, and stews. Palm oil and other vegetable oils – namely, coconut and groundnut oils – are used to prepare dishes. Though all of these oils make delicious traditional meals, palm oil is the most commonly used, particularly, for cooking mixed sauces. The palm fruit produces two types of oil: palm oil and palm kernel oil.

Palm Oil: For generations, palm oil has been extracted from the palm fruit of palm trees that grow in the wild. These trees grow very tall, and getting the fruit involves the difficult and sometimes hazardous task of climbing these immensely tall trees. To increase production of palm oil, a new palm tree variety was introduced – it is shorter, grows faster, and the fruit is fleshier with little to no nut. As a result, they are easier to harvest. Whereas the oil from the palm tree is reddish in color and very fluid, with a water-like consistency, this new variety is not as red or as fluid. When people talk about the high cholesterol components of palm oil, most West Africans attribute this to the palm oil in the latter category. West Africans still view the original palm oil as being very healthy; just as healthy as it has been for so many generations. However, the original palm oils are gradually disappearing because of the difficulty associated with the production. This gives way to the variety that is easier to produce. When available, the original (and healthier) palm oil tastes better, but is more expensive.

Palm Kernel Oil: Palm kernel oil is different from palm oil. While the former has a cream color, the latter is red. Moreover, palm kernel oil is produced from the nuts of the palm fruit. It is rarely used for cooking, but is mostly used in the production of soap. Other types of vegetable oils are used in the preparation of some soups, stews and mixed sauces.

Nuts: Though there are a wide variety of nuts, it is the kola nut, groundnut, and palm kernel nut that many West Africans believe to have originated from West Africa.

The **kola nut** is valued both for its role as a stimulant and for its customary role in social events. It is an energizer that can also prevent one from feeling hungry. It is always used during weddings, naming ceremonies, funerals, and memorial ceremonies. The dye from the nut is used in the production of tie-dye clothes. Long ago, it was believed to possess medicinal values, such as reducing labor pains, treating swollen fresh wounds, and remedying some parasitic infections.

Palm nut, derived from the kernel of the palm fruit, has a very hard shell. Perhaps it is rarely eaten because chewing it can be so difficult. However, it is a useful export: the oil extracted from this nut is used in the making of soap, both inside and outside the region. Though rare, the oil also can be used for cooking vegetables.

Groundnuts (or peanuts) are very popular. They can be eaten as snacks or used as an ingredient in cooking meals. Roasted groundnuts and raw peanuts, boiled in its shell with a little bit of salt, make great snacks. Groundnut paste is frequently used in the preparation of many dishes.

Benniseed, commonly known outside the region as sesame seed, is also eaten. When toasted and ground, it can be used to flavor dishes. It can also be toasted and mixed with sugar to produce a lovely snack called *benniseed* cake. Likewise, oil extracted from this seed can be used in cooking some dishes. Like groundnuts, *benniseed* is believed to be very rich in vitamins.

Bor-boueh and **tola** are nuts from two different types of bush mango trees and are classified as vegetables in Sierra Leone. In Nigeria, *bor-boueh* is known as *ogbornor*. The seeds from both nuts can be dried after harvesting and subsequently ground in powder form. Although they still grow in the wild, they are now increasingly available in Asian and other ethnic food stores. When cooked, their powder transforms into a very tasty dish that has a slightly slippery consistency and an appearance similar to a thick curry soup. Each seed powder still retains its respective and unique fruity and nutty flavor. Other seeds include the *egusi* or melon seed, which can be dried, ground, and used to thicken soups and vegetables. They are usually available ready-made in food markets in the region. Outside the region, they are available in Asian and other ethnic food stores.

Spices and Herbs: There are a large variety of hot peppers and spices available in the region. Grains of Paradise is one spice that is believed to be indigenous to West Africa. However, several other spices and herbs, like bird chili, habanero peppers, scotch bonnet chili, ginger, garlic, cloves, bay leaves, cinnamon, and parsley, arrived in West Africa from other countries. They are now grown in West Africa and are used particularly to prepare some types of soups and stews and to season food. Further, there is also a type of herb that grows wild in Sierra Leone called *paw-paw-daah*. It has a keenly unique smell that is very different from many other spices. It gives sea fish, freshwater fish, and shellfish dishes an exceptionally tasty and yummy flavor.

Planning and Preparing Ahead

There are some ingredients that take longer to cook because they have to be cooked until they are soft and tender. To save time on cooking, and to enjoy preparing meals, it is always a good idea to prepare some ingredients in advance. In particular, it is a good idea to boil meat, free-range chicken, game, smoked fish, or beans ahead of time. Most of these protein items are, by their nature, very hard. They must be cooked until tender to achieve the right taste. Since the process of getting it tender takes a longer time, I suggest you plan the family meal for a whole week and then boil all the protein ingredients, for all the meals, before the week starts. This preparation will save you time. Divide the meat into portions to match the number of times it will be cooked during the week. Preserve the precooked meat in individually marked bowls and refrigerate. Consequently, at cooking time, all you have to do is add the tender meat to the other ingredients in the pot. This does not only apply to meats, but to all the proteins mentioned earlier, including the smoked fish and beans. Of course, boil and refrigerate these separately.

To save even more time, I recommend that you use a pressure cooker to boil the proteins. Cooking any food item until it is tender can take 1 to 2 hours, if using an ordinary pot; it takes only 30 to 40 minutes, if using a pressure cooker. The information below details the methods to prepare protein ingredients.

BOILING METHODS: Boiled meat, poultry, and/or beans are required for cooking soups, stews, and mixed sauces. Stocks can also be prepared using the boiling method. A good stock helps to make a dish delicious.

Meat and Game: These have to be boiled until they are soft and tender. To boil meat:

1. Trim and cut meat into serving pieces. Put into a bowl, wash, and drain off water.
2. Add salt and Maggi, to taste, and stir together so that the salt and Maggi blend in evenly.
3. Add to a large pot and bring to a boil in its own liquid over high heat.
4. Reduce heat to medium and continue to cook until liquid around meat evaporates. Taste and add more salt if desired.
5. Then add enough water to cover meat (about 6 inches above meat). Cover and bring to a boil over high heat.
6. Continue to cook until water completely evaporates and meat is soft and tender. If necessary, add more water and continue to cook until meat is soft and tender.

Cooking time can vary between 1 to 2 hours. But for a shorter time frame, you have the option of cooking the meat in a pressure cooker.

Quantity of water added and cooking time varies depending on the type of meat. You should, however, be able to gauge when the meat is done.

To boil meat using a pressure cooker:

1. Trim and cut meat into serving pieces. Put into a bowl, wash, and drain off water.
2. Add salt and Maggi, to taste, and stir together so that the salt and Maggi blend in evenly.
3. Put into a pressure cooker and add water (about 3 inches above meat).
4. Cover and cook on high heat for 20 to 30 minutes.

I also suggest that you consult the instructions on your pressure cooker.

Meat keeps and tastes better if you allow it to cook until all the liquid evaporates. This means that the seasoning will be trapped inside the meat even as it cooks later with vegetables or as soups and stews. After boiling the meat until it is tender, store it in the refrigerator and use for cooking when ready. If you can't wait for all the liquid to evaporate, keep the meat in the stock and refrigerate. It will get tender and absorb the seasoning as it stays in the refrigerator. Use meat and stock for cooking when ready. Use the stock or top it up with water where a recipe calls for water.

Poultry including Domesticated Fowl or Game Birds: These can be boiled using the same method used above for the "meat and game." Broilers chickens are soft and do not have to be cooked in advance.

Broilers: This type of chicken is not as hard as the domesticated or game fowls. Broilers are easy to cook and are very tasty in soups and stews. To prepare this type of chicken:

1. Chop chicken into serving pieces. Remove the skin and discard. Put chicken into a bowl. (In West African dishes, broilers do not taste good if the skin is left on.)
2. Add cold water, wash, and drain off water.
3. Add salt and Maggi, to taste, and stir together so that the salt and Maggi blend in evenly.
4. Add to a pot, cover, and bring to a boil over medium heat in its own liquid.
5. Reduce heat and simmer until all of its juices completely evaporate.
6. Fry chicken in vegetable oil. Set aside and use for cooking at the appropriate time.

Beans: To save time, I recommend that you soak the beans in cold water for a few hours or overnight before boiling. To boil beans:

1. Place beans into a large bowl and pick through to discard any floating grains or bean skin.
2. Wash with cold water to make sure it is very clean. (This is particularly important when cooking black-eyed beans because the water in which it is boiled is used as stock for cooking black-eyed beans sauce.)
3. Add to a pot and cover with water (four times more water than the quantity of beans).
4. Bring to a boil over high heat. Continue to cook for 40 minutes, adding more water if necessary to cook the beans until soft and tender.

5. For beans, other than black-eyed beans, drain off hot water. Wash with cold water. (For black-eyed beans, it is recommended that you keep the beans in the water in which it is boiled, as this is the main stock for cooking your black-eyed beans later.)

6. Remove the eyes (the black part at the end of the beans), rinse, and keep refrigerated until required for cooking.

Black-Eyed Beans: For the preparation of **Beans Akara** and **Oleleh**

1. Place beans into a large bowl and pick through to discard any floating grains or bean skin.

2. Wash with cold water to make sure it is very clean. Drain off water and return the beans to the bowl.

3. Pour boiling water over beans to cover (at least 6 inches). Keep beans in water for 20 minutes. (This will cause the skin and black eyes to detach and, therefore, make them easier to remove.)

4. Drain off hot water. Rub beans vigorously between your palms and then against the bowl with your palms. Repeat several times until the black eyes and most of the skin falls off. Rub the beans that still have their skin and/or eyes between your thumb and forefinger. Repeat until all the beans are skinless.

5. Add cold water to the skinless beans. Stir and rotate the bowl several times to allow the remaining skin and eyes to settle on top. Drain off water, along with the skin and eyes.

6. Rinse the skinless beans and then drain with a colander. Repeat with the rest of the beans, processing a little at a time until all the beans are clean and cream white in color. Refrigerate the clean beans until you are ready to use.

Stock: To prepare poultry, meat, or game stock:

1. Remove the parts of the poultry, meat, or game that may not be of much use while cooking a meal. (For poultry, I usually use the backbone; for meat or game, I use the hard, boney parts that are not likely to get soft, even after being boiled for a lengthy time.)

2. Take about 2¼ pounds of these parts, wash them, and remove any fat. Rinse and add to a pot. Add salt, to taste.

3. Mix in large slices from 1 large fresh onion, a bit of pepper (optional), and 1 small Maggi cube.

4. Add 10 to 12 cups of water and bring to a boil over high heat. Continue to cook for 1½ hours or until water goes down by half.

5. Reduce heat and simmer for 30 minutes. Remove and allow to cool. Then, remove any excess fat that may surface to the top of the liquid. Sieve and store stock in the refrigerator until you are ready to use. (If preparing using a pressure cooker, the stock will be ready after only 30 minutes of cooking.)

Hot Pepper Sauce: This is a very handy accompaniment to have in your fridge. This sauce can be served alongside boiled or fried roots, tubers, and tree crops. You can also add this sauce to soups and stews. (See recipe in the *Snacks and Accompaniments* chapter.)

Raw Fish: Fish is in excellent, fresh condition when it has firm fins, tight scales, bright red gills, and clear eyes with very black pupils and, most importantly, a fresh smell. To prepare fish:

1. Clean fish by removing the scales, gills, internal parts, fins, and tails. Then wash well with cold water. (If possible, get your fishmonger to clean your fish for you.)
2. Place fish on a cutting board and cut into serving pieces.
3. If you prefer to keep the fish whole, place it on a cutting board and make 3 deep, diagonal cuts, of an estimated equal distance from each other. Make these cuts on each side of the fish. Rinse the fish.
4. Squeeze juice from lime over the fish, whether it is whole or cut into pieces. Generously rub the lime juice all over the fish, and then drain off the lime juice from the fish.
5. Pack into refrigerator bags and preserve in freezer.

Raw Herring: These can be prepared whole by following the directions for raw fish *(see the (Raw Fish) recipe above).* They can also be deboned and cooked in stews or served as snacks. To prepare as snacks:

1. Clean herring by taking off scales and cleaning inside. Remove head and throw it away.
2. Cut a ring around the point where the tail joins the trunk of the fish. Squeeze fish gently on the sides. This will detach flesh from bone.
3. With two fingers of each hand, hold the fish tight at the point of the ring. Draw the fish, with the fingers facing the body of the fish, and pull towards the head while holding firmly on the tail end. This will remove the central bone structure of the fish.
4. Rinse the flesh and cut into serving sizes. Put the fish into a bowl. Season with lime, garlic, and Maggi. Marinate for 30 minutes.
5. Heat oil in a skillet and fry the fish. Put the fried fish in bowl and refrigerate.

Smoked Fish: To prepare:

1. Wash smoked fish thoroughly and place into a pot. Add salt, to taste. Add water to cover surface by 2 inches.
2. Bring to a boil and cook until tender. Cooking time can vary between 20 to 30 minutes, depending on type and size of fish.
3. Remove from pot and allow to cool. Remove the bones and break the smoked fish's flesh into large flakes. (Smaller smoked fish can be flaked into very small pieces. They blend well with large fish flakes and other protein ingredients in mixed sauces.)
4. Keep refrigerated until required for cooking.

Ogiri, Dried Crayfish, Dried Shrimp, and Kenda: These are all condiments used to infuse dishes with a distinctive aroma.

Ogiri is made from fermented *benniseed* and sold ready-made in the markets in many West African countries. Its aroma is similar to a particular smoked crayfish known as *fasei* in Sierra Leone. In the rural south and east of Sierra Leone, dried crayfish is used more often than *ogiri*. *Kenda*, a fermented fruit seed, is another aroma-yielding condiment, which is widely used in the northern parts of Sierra Leone. The plant from which it is produced grows mainly in the north, whereas the source plant for *ogiri* grows mainly in the south and the east. Both *ogiri* and *kenda* are available in the urban areas. In regions where *ogiri* or *kenda* are not available, powdered, dried crayfish or powdered, dried shrimp can be used as a substitute for the aroma associated with *ogiri*. Crayfish, however, is a closer substitute for *ogiri* than dried shrimp.

Powdered, dried crayfish and powdered, dried shrimp are available in Asian and other ethnic food stores in many countries.

To prepare dried crayfish or dried shrimp:

1. Put the dried crayfish (or shrimp) into a large bowl. Pick through to make sure that it is very clean.
2. Grind using a blender or a mortar and pestle and then sieve.
3. Keep the powdered, dried crayfish (or shrimp) in a jar and store in its dry state.
4. Use for cooking at the appropriate time.

Egusi: We get *egusi* from a special variety of melon seeds grown in West Africa. *Egusi* is usually available ready-made in West African markets. In countries outside the region, it is available in Asian and other ethnic food stores. However, if you only have the seeds available dry and grind them into a fine powder. Keep the *egusi* in an airtight jar and use to cook when needed.

Groundnut Paste or Peanut Butter: Peanut is commonly known as groundnut in West Africa. For cooking purposes, I suggest the easier option of using the ready-made natural peanut butter – i.e. peanut butter that uses only peanut or peanut with salt ingredients.

Sodium Bicarbonate (Lubi): *Lubi* is a type of sodium bicarbonate produced locally with local materials, mostly in the rural areas of various countries in the region. For many generations, *lubi* has been used in cooking certain dishes in Sierra Leone and other West African countries. However, a new product called bicarbonate of soda has replaced *lubi* in many areas. It is readily available in food stores, and like *lubi*, bicarbonate of soda helps to maintain the green color in vegetables, even after cooking. Also, a little pinch of it can enhance the texture of vegetables like okra and *crain-crain*, and make harder vegetables, like okra leaves and *pillaah*, softer and greener when they are cooked.

To get the green effect on non-slippery vegetables:

1. Add a teaspoon of the bicarbonate of soda to a large bowl of water. (The volume of water should be about three times the quantity of the vegetable used.)
2. Wash the vegetable in the bicarbonate mixture and drain.
3. Add cold water, rinse and drain before cooking.

To soften vegetables and maintain their green color, add a small pinch of bicarbonate of soda, mix well, and cook. To make vegetables, like okra, okra leaves, or *crain-crain*, green and slippery, add a small pinch of *lubi* or sodium bicarbonate, mix well, and cook.

Do not use too much *lubi* or bicarbonate of soda on any vegetable. A little at a time is good enough to maintain the quality and appearance of the vegetable. In fact, too much of either will have the opposite effect.

Some carbohydrate type foods: From left cocoyam, green and ripe plantains, yams.

Country Rice (Uncooked)

More Carbohydrate type foods: At bottom, sweet potatoes, center, green and ripe plantains, top right, cassava, top left, yams.

Other vegetables that can be made into traditional vegetables. From left, Italian spinach, Swiss chard and collard green.

Cassava Leaves

Scotch Bonnet Pepper

Potato leaves (whole and chopped)

Crain-Crain

Okra Leaves

Okra (whole and chopped)

Various types of garden eggs. Garden eggs on left and right used to cook soups, okra sauces, potato leaf sauces and vegetarian type vegetables. Garden eggs on top used mainly for cooking cassava leaf sauces, okra and broad beans dishes.

Other types of garden eggs. These are used for cooking soups, okra, potato leaf and other vegetarian type dishes.

Various eggplants

Young pillaah with its related garden eggs

Old pillaah and its related garden eggs

Recipes and Food-Related Stories

In between the recipes, I have included a collection of food-related stories that I believe you, your family, and your friends will find interesting. The recipes are organized under the headings of *Main Dishes, Snacks and Accompaniments, Tropical Fruits* and *Beverages.* The *Main Dishes* are separated into soups, stews, mixed sauces with their vegetarian variations, and grains including rice, tubers, and tree crops. Although West African meals do not traditionally come with appetizers and desserts, I have incorporated a variety of snacks that can serve as appetizers and desserts for those who may prefer to have these with their meals.

Note: Choice of Pepper

Throughout the recipes in this book, I have listed pepper as one of the ingredients. For the optimal flavor of the dishes, the best pepper to choose is a very hot type, like habanero or scotch bonnet pepper. If you choose to use any other pepper, it is best to measure for a taste that is as hot as you can handle.

Main Dishes: Pepper Soups and Light Soups

PEPPER SOUP: This soup does not have to be cooked with a lot of pepper. Depending on your preference, the amount of pepper added can range from none to moderate to a lot. You may choose to add either fresh ground pepper or a whole pepper. Adding a whole pepper to pepper soup (and even any other soup or mixed sauce), gives the dish an alluring aroma, without absorbing all of the pepper's hot taste. Whenever I cook, if the pepper available to me is very hot, like habanero or scotch bonnet, I cook it whole in the soup, which gives the dish a nice aroma. If you like a very hot soup, mash enough pepper into the soup until you get the desired hotness.

Pepper soup can be cooked with one type of meat or an assortment of meats. You can combine beef, oxtail, goat, or even the edible internal organs of the meat to make a great pepper soup. Also, it can be prepared as a seafood pepper soup by using only the fish or by combining it with other ingredients, like shrimp or oysters, to make an equally delightful pepper soup. What I love about pepper soup is its dual role: as a good remedy for the sick or its ability to keep you warm on a rainy day. It is known to have the capacity to "pepper" up one's system when one's body needs it most.

Pepper soup is very popular during a party. It is a good remedy for hangovers. It is usually served halfway through a party around midnight after guests have had many drinks. This is, purportedly, to prevent people from feeling drunk. Understandably, fish pepper soup is never served at parties: it would be challenging to serve fish that has bones to someone who is already drunk. Oxtail, meat, or pig's trotters pepper soups are more popular because it is impossible to swallow the bones even when one is drunk. Pepper soup can be served with or without boiled tubers.

For those who like to start their meals with appetizers, pepper soup served without boiled tubers is very suitable.

LIGHT SOUPS: Light soups, on the other hand, are thicker than pepper soups. The ingredients for this type of soup consist of vegetables and other ingredients that are not added to pepper soup. Some of these ingredients like eggplant, garlic and fish flakes give the soup a thicker appearance and a unique lip-smacking taste. Light soups go very well with steamed rice, couscous, *fufu* (made from fermented cassava), and *tuei* (made from cassava flour) and also other various types of fufu. (See the *(Main Dishes) Tubers and Tree Crops Dishes chapter*) There are also light soups made with meat, chicken, and fresh fish.

Pepper Soups and Light Soups

Pepper Soup   Oxtail Pepper Soup
Variation: Oxtail plus Pig's Trotters
Pig's Trotters Pepper Soup
Variation: Pig's Trotters prepared with Other Meats
Halal/Kosher Pepper Soup
Chicken Pepper Soup
Variation: Free-Range Fowl/Game Bird
Fresh Fish Pepper Soup
Fish Fillet and Shellfish Pepper Soup

Light Soup   Meat Light Soup
Chicken Light Soup
Variation: Free-Range Fowl/Game Bird
Fresh Fish Light Soup

OXTAIL PEPPER SOUP

SERVES 6

INGREDIENTS

24 bite-size pieces of oxtail
1 plus ¼ teaspoon salt or to taste
2 small or 1 large Maggi cube
8 cups water or enough to boil
    oxtail until tender
2 cups plus 3 cups water
1 medium onion, finely chopped
1 to 2 hot peppers, ground or
    whole (optional)
1medium fresh tomato, finely
    chopped
2 teaspoons tomato purée

Oxtail plus pig's trotters pepper soup served with boiled yam

1. Season oxtail with 1 teaspoon salt and 1 small or ½ large Maggi. Put into a large pot, cover and bring to a boil over medium heat. Continue to cook for 10 minutes or until most of the water evaporates.
2. Add 8 cups water and cook over high heat adding more water if needed to cook until oxtail is very tender but not broken. (If possible, use a pressure cooker.)
3. Add 2 cups water, and bring to a boil. Add onion, pepper, and tomatoes. Cover, and continue to cook for 5 to 10 minutes.
4. Add the remaining 3 cups water, tomato purée and the rest of the Maggi and salt, cover and bring to a boil. Taste and add more salt if desired.
5. Reduce heat to low and simmer for 5 to 10 minutes.

Serve hot with boiled tuber (like cassava, potato, cocoyam, or yam) or with tree crop (like boiled plantain or boiled green banana). To eat, drop the tuber or tree crop into the soup bowl and drink.

Variation: Oxtail Plus Pig's Trotters: Follow cooking procedure for *Oxtail Pepper Soup*, but, reduce the 24 bite-size pieces oxtail by 12 and add instead 12 bite-size pieces of pig's trotters. Boil oxtail and pig's trotters separately until both are tender. (See recipe for *Pig's Trotters Pepper Soup* for information on how to boil pig's trotters until tender.) When cooking this soup, add both oxtail and pig's trotters at the point where the oxtail recipe calls for 2 cups of water.

PIG'S TROTTERS PEPPER SOUP: This soup can be cooked using only pig's trotters or combined with other meats. Pig's trotters are sold fresh or preserved. More salt is required to cook fresh pig's trotters. The preserved ones are already salted and processed, and taste better in pepper soup. They are usually pinkish in color.

If using preserved, salted pig's trotters, soak it in a large bowl of cold water for a few hours after cutting it into pieces. Drain off water, add to a pot of cold water, and cook until it is soft. After cooking, rinse in cold water to remove the salt and excess fat. Unpreserved pig's trotters are not salty and therefore do not have to be soaked in water before boiling. The recipe below is for the salted and processed pig's trotters when cooked with other types of meat.

SERVES 6

INGREDIENTS

6 pig's trotters, cut along joints into
    biting pieces, boiled until tender (use
    pressure cooker, if possible)
6 cups water
¼ teaspoon salt or to taste
1 medium onion, finely chopped
1 medium fresh tomatoes, finely
    chopped
2 teaspoons tomato purée
1 small Maggi cube
1 to 2 hot peppers, ground or whole
    (optional)

Pig's trotters pepper soup

1. Discard stock from pig's trotters. Put the pig's trotters and 6 cups water into a large pot.
2. Add salt, onion, tomatoes, tomato puree, Maggi and pepper.
3. Cover, bring to a boil over high heat and continue to cook for 15 minutes.
4. Taste and add more salt if desired. Reduce heat to low and simmer for 10 minutes.

Serve hot with boiled tuber (like cassava, potato, cocoyam, or yam) or with tree crop (like boiled plantain or boiled green banana). To eat, drop the tuber or tree crop into the soup bowl and drink.

Variation: Pig's Trotters prepared with Other Meats: Follow cooking procedure for *Pig's Trotters Pepper Soup* but reduce the pig's trotters to 3 and add 1 pound of any type of meat such as beef on the bone, goat, or game. Boil meat and pig's trotters separately until both are tender. (See recipe for *Pig's Trotters Pepper Soup* for information on how to boil pig's trotters until tender.) When cooking this pepper soup, add meat and pig's trotters at the same time.

HALAL/KOSHER PEPPER SOUP: Any kind of meat can be used to cook this soup: steak, beef on bone, goat, or chosen game meat. You can use one type of meat or combine one or two meats in the same soup.

SERVES 6

INGREDIENTS

1½ pounds meat, stewing steak, brisket, or other parts of any meat, cut into serving cubes
½ teaspoon salt or to taste
1 small Maggi cube
4 plus 4 cups water
1 medium onion, finely chopped
1 to 2 hot peppers, ground or whole (optional)
1 medium fresh tomato, finely chopped
2 teaspoons tomato purée

1. Wash meat, drain off water, Season with salt and Maggi and put into a pot.
2. Over medium heat, bring meat to a boil and continue to cook for 10 minutes or until most of the liquid evaporates.
3. Add 4 cups water and bring to a boil over high heat. Continue to cook adding more water if needed to soften meat. Cook until most of the water evaporates and meat is tender.
4. Add the balance 4 cups water, onion, pepper, chopped tomato and tomato puree and bring to a boil.
5. Taste and add more salt if desired. Reduce heat to low and simmer for 10 to 15 minutes.

Serve hot with boiled tuber (like cassava, potato, cocoyam, or yam) or with tree crop (like boiled plantain or boiled green banana). To eat, drop the tuber or tree crop into the soup bowl and drink.

CHICKEN PEPPER SOUP

SERVES 6

INGREDIENTS

1 large broiler chicken (2½ to 3 pounds)
½ tablespoon salt or to taste
1 small Maggi cube
1 tablespoon vegetable oil
1 medium onion, chopped into large cubes
4 cups water
1 to 2 hot peppers, ground or whole (optional)
1 medium fresh tomatoes, chopped
1 tablespoon tomato purée

1. Cut chicken into bite-size pieces. Remove the skin and discard. Put chicken into a bowl, rinse with cold water, and drain off water. Season with salt and Maggi.
2. Put chicken into a large skillet. Cover, bring to a boil over medium heat and continue to cook until all the liquid around the chicken evaporates.
3. Reduce heat to low. Continue to cook in the dry pot that will now be slightly oily with the chicken's oil, turning chicken pieces frequently from side to side until slightly brown on all sides. Remove from heat and set aside.
4. Put oil into a large pot and place over medium heat. Add onion and sauté until soft and shiny. Add chicken, 4 cups water, pepper, fresh tomatoes and tomato puree. Cover, bring to a boil and continue to cook for 10 minutes.
5. Taste and add more salt if desired. Reduce heat to low and simmer for 10 to 15 minutes.

Serve hot with boiled tuber (like cassava, potato, cocoyam, or yam) or with tree crop (like boiled plantain or boiled green banana). To eat, drop the tuber or tree crop into the soup bowl and drink.

Variation: Free-Range Fowl/Game Bird: This soup comes with its own unique, delectable flavor, quite different from the delicious broiler chicken pepper soup.

SERVES 6

INGREDIENTS

1 large free-range fowl or game bird (2½ to 3 pounds)
½ tablespoon salt or to taste
1 small Maggi cube
6 cups water or enough to boil chicken until tender
4 cups water
1 medium onion, chopped
1 to 2 hot peppers, ground or whole (optional)
1 medium fresh tomatoes, chopped
1 tablespoon tomato purée

1. Cut chicken into bite-size pieces, but do not remove skin unless you prefer it skinless. Wash, drain, and put chicken into a bowl. Season with salt and Maggi and put into a large pot.
2. Cover, bring to a boil over medium heat and continue to cook for 5 minutes or until the liquid around the chicken evaporates.
3. Add 6 cups water. Cover and continue to cook adding more water if needed to cook chicken until tender. (If possible, use pressure cooker to cook chicken until tender. Do not use 6 cups water but just enough to cover chicken by 2 inches.)
4. Add 4 cups water, onion, pepper, fresh tomatoes and tomato puree. Cover, bring to a boil and cook for 10 minutes.
5. Taste and add more salt if desired. Reduce heat to low and simmer for 10 to 15 minutes.

Serve hot with boiled tuber (like cassava, potato, cocoyam, or yam) or with tree crop (like boiled plantain or boiled green banana). To eat, drop the tuber or tree crop into the soup bowl and drink.

FRESH FISH PEPPER SOUP: This soup can be cooked using fresh, whole fish or fish fillet.

SERVES 6

INGREDIENTS

3 medium-size fresh, whole tilapia or snapper
2 limes
½ teaspoon salt or to taste
1 small Maggi cube
1 tablespoon vegetable oil
2 medium onions, chopped into large cubes
1 to 2 hot peppers, ground or whole (optional)
1 medium fresh tomato, finely chopped
1 tablespoon tomato purée
4 cups water

1. Clean fish and cut into 12 serving pieces. Rinse and put into a bowl. Squeeze juice from limes and pour over fish. Rub the lime juice all over the fish and then drain off lime juice.
2. Season with salt and Maggi. Put fish into a large pot and steam over low heat. Remove pot from heat and set aside.
3. In a skillet, heat oil over medium heat. Add onions and sauté until soft and shiny. Add pepper, fresh tomatoes, tomato puree and 4 cups water. Bring to a boil.
4. Pour content in skillet into pot over simmered fish and bring to a boil over medium heat.
5. Taste and add more salt if desired. Reduce heat to low and simmer for 5 to 10 minutes.

Serve hot with boiled tuber (like cassava, potato, cocoyam, or yam) or with tree crop (like boiled plantain or boiled green banana). To eat, drop the tuber or tree crop into the soup bowl and drink.

FISH FILLET AND SHELLFISH PEPPER SOUP: For this soup, use all the ingredients for the fish pepper soup, except the 3 medium-size whole fish. Replace the whole fish with fish fillet and assemble the ingredients listed below.

SERVES 6

INGREDIENTS

8 halves fish fillet, tilapia, or snapper
1 lime
½ teaspoon salt
½ cup shrimp, cleaned, deveined, and steamed
¼ cup oyster, cleaned and steamed (optional)
1 tablespoon cooking oil
1 medium onion, chopped
1 medium fresh tomatoes, finely chopped
1 to 2 hot peppers, ground or whole (optional)
1 small Maggi cube
1 teaspoon tomato purée
4 cups water

1. Cut fish into serving pieces and put into a bowl. Wash with cold water and then drain off water. Squeeze juice from lime, pour over fish, rub lime juice all over fish and then drain off lime juice.
2. Season fish with salt, put into a large pot, and steam over low heat. Remove from heat. Add steamed shrimp and oysters. Cover and set aside.
3. In a skillet, heat oil over medium heat. Add onions and sauté until soft and shiny. Add chopped tomatoes, pepper, maggi, tomato puree and 4 cups water. Cover and bring to a boil.
4. Pour content in the skillet into pot over simmered fish, shrimp, and oyster. Bring to a boil over medium heat. Taste and add more salt if desired. Reduce heat to low and simmer for 5 to 10 minutes.

Serve hot with boiled tuber (like cassava, potato, cocoyam, or yam) or with tree crop (like boiled plantain or boiled green banana). To eat, drop the tuber or tree crop into the soup bowl and drink.

MEAT LIGHT SOUP: Any kind of meat can be used to cook this soup: steak, beef on bone, goat, or game meat. You can use one type of meat or use an assortment of meats in the same soup.

SERVES 6

INGREDIENTS

1 pound meat, stewing steak or beef on bone or any other meat, cut into serving pieces
½ teaspoon salt or to taste
1 small Maggi cube
6 plus 4 cups water
1 medium onion, chopped into large quarter sections
1 small eggplant, peeled, chopped into large cubes, and seeds removed.
1 medium fresh tomato, chopped into two halves
½ cup smoked fish flakes (optional)
2 cloves garlic
1 teaspoon tomato puree
1 to 2 hot peppers, ground or whole (optional)

1. Put meat into a bowl, wash, and drain off water. Season with salt and Maggi and add to a large pot. Over medium heat, bring to a boil. Reduce heat to low and continue to cook for 10 minutes.
2. Add 6 cups water and cook over high heat adding more water if needed to soften meat slightly. Add onion, eggplant, tomato, fish flakes, and garlic. Cover and continue to cook until meat and fish are tender and vegetables are soft.
3. Remove pot from heat and put contents into a bowl. Separate meat and stock from all other ingredients. Return meat and stock to pot and reduce heat to medium.
4. Meanwhile, purée all the other boiled ingredients using a blender or mortar and pestle.
5. Add the pureed vegetables and all the other ingredients to the pot, cover and bring to a boil. Taste and add more salt if desired. Reduce heat to low and simmer for 15 minutes.

Serve hot with boiled tuber (like cassava, potato, cocoyam, or yam) or with tree crop (like boiled plantain or boiled green banana). To eat, drop the tuber or tree crop into the soup bowl and drink.

CHICKEN LIGHT SOUP

SERVES 6

INGREDIENTS

1 large broiler chicken (2½ to 3 pounds)
½ teaspoon salt or to taste
1 small Maggi cube
3 plus 2 cups water
1 medium onion, chopped into large quarter sections
1 small eggplant, peeled, chopped into small cubes and seeds removed
1 large fresh tomato, chopped into two halves
½ cup smoked fish flakes (optional)
2 cloves garlic
1 teaspoon tomato purée
1 to 2 hot peppers ground or whole (optional)

1. Cut chicken into serving pieces. Remove the skin and discard. Put chicken into a bowl, rinse with cold water and drain off water.
2. Season with salt and Maggi and add to a large pot. Cover and simmer over low heat. Add 3 cups water, onion, eggplant, tomato, fish flakes, and garlic. Cover and cook over high heat until vegetables are very soft. Remove pot from heat and separate chicken and stock from all other ingredients.
3. Return chicken and stock to pot and continue to cook. Meanwhile, purée all the other boiled ingredients using a blender or mortar and pestle. Add to the pot, cover and bring to a boil.
4. Taste and add more salt if desired. Reduce heat to low and simmer for 10 to15 minutes.

Serve hot with boiled tuber (like cassava, potato, cocoyam, or yam) or with tree crop (like boiled plantain or boiled green banana). To eat, drop the tuber or tree crop into the soup bowl and drink.

Variation: Free-Range Fowl/Game Bird: Using the recipe above, replace the broiler chicken with a free-range fowl or game bird. These birds, unlike broiler chicken, can be cooked with their skins on. And, because they are harder than broiler chickens, add enough water to allow it to cook for a longer period until soft and tender.

FRESH FISH LIGHT SOUP

SERVES 6

INGREDIENTS

3 medium-size fresh, whole tilapia or snapper
2 limes
½ teaspoon salt or to taste
1 small Maggi cube
2 plus 4 cups water
1 medium onion, chopped into large quarter sections
1 small eggplant, peeled, chopped into large cubes and seeds removed
1 large fresh tomato, chopped into two halves
½ cup smoked fish flakes (optional)
2 cloves garlic
1 teaspoon tomato puree
1 to 2 hot peppers, ground or whole (optional)

1. Clean fish and cut into 12 serving pieces. Rinse and put into a bowl. Squeeze juice from limes and pour over fish. Rub the lime juice all over the fish, and then drain off lime juice.
2. Season fish with salt and Maggi. Put into a large pot and simmer over low heat for 15 minutes. Remove pot from heat and put aside.
3. Add 2 cups water, onion, eggplant, fresh tomato, fish flakes, and garlic to a medium pot. Cover and cook over high heat until vegetables are very soft. Remove pot from heat.
4. Purée the softened vegetables and fish flakes using a blender or mortar and pestle. Add to the fish in the pot.
5. Add remaining water or any leftover liquid from the boiled vegetables. Bring to a boil over high heat. Add tomato puree and pepper and continue to cook for 5 minutes.
6. Taste and add more salt if desired. Reduce heat to low and simmer for 15 minutes.

Serve hot with boiled tuber (like cassava, potato, cocoyam, or yam) or with tree crop (like boiled plantain or boiled green banana). To eat, drop the tuber or tree crop into the soup bowl and drink.

Groundnut, Egusi, Palm Oil, and Other Soups

Whenever I invite people to my home for the first time, groundnut soup is always a must on the menu. It is a soup I always put on the table with great confidence, no matter who the guest may be. It is simple to prepare, and I have never met anyone who has tasted it and refused to give it a score of one hundred percent. I think this is because the ingredients (particularly the groundnut paste are less mysterious and more universal than those in other West African dishes. *Groundnut soup, and other soups covered in this chapter, can be made with goat, beef, game meat, fish, poultry, and free-range fowl/game birds.* They can also be made with a combination of different types of seafood and fresh water foods. When cooked as groundnut soup, fresh fish or smoked fish can be very mouth-watering. For those who love vegetarian dishes, these soups can be prepared using the same recipes, but by replacing the meat or fish with plenty of mushrooms or a larger portion of eggplants or your favorite vegetables.

Groundnuts, also known as peanuts, can be made into paste and added to soups, stews, and some types of mixed *palaver* sauces. They are popular across the region because of the unique, delightful, and nutty taste that they give to several types of dishes. Groundnut paste is available in stores labeled as peanut butter. For the recipes in this book, I recommend the use of natural peanut butter, which usually has its ingredients limited to peanuts or peanuts with salt. To avoid unwelcome results, never use peanut butter that contains sugar (as my son learned the hard way many years ago! – but that story is for another book).

Egusi: This comes from the seeds of a creeping melon plant that is grown in West Africa. The seeds are dried and ground. *Egusi* is available ready-made in West African markets and in Asian and other ethnic food stores outside the region. Like groundnuts, it is used in soups and some types of mixed vegetables like bitter leaves, sorrel leaves, or sorrel flowers. It is a very popular ingredient because it gives a sauce a specific creaminess, while also infusing it with a unique, nutty flavor.

Benniseed or Sesame Seed: These can be dried, roasted, and ground into powder form. *Benniseed* is available all over the world.

Palm Oil: This is used as a main ingredient for cooking some types of soups, stews, and mixed sauces.

Groundnut, Egusi, Palm Oil, and Other Soups

Groundnut Soup Beef Groundnut Soup
Chicken Groundnut Soup
Pork Groundnut Soup
Fisherman's Groundnut Soup

Egusi *Egusi* Soup

Palm Oil Fresh Fish Palm Oil Soup

Benniseed Fish *Benniseed*/Sesame Soup

Food Story Sisterhood Emerging through Cooking

BEEF GROUNDNUT SOUP: This recipe can also be used to cook various types of meat, such as beef, oxtail, stewing steak, beef on bone, pork, pig's trotters, goat, or game meat. Adjust quantity of meat to suit your needs.

SERVES 6

INGREDIENTS

2 pounds beef
½ plus ¼ teaspoon salt or to taste
1 large or 2 small Maggi cubes
4 cups plus 3 cups water
2 tablespoons groundnut paste
2 medium eggplants, peeled, chopped into small chunks and seeds removed.
2 garden eggs (optional) stalk removed, whole or chopped into large pieces.
1 medium onion, finely chopped
1 to 2 hot peppers, ground or whole (optional)
1 large fresh tomato, finely chopped
1 tablespoon tomato purée

1. Cut beef into serving pieces. Put into a bowl, wash, and drain off water. Season with ½ teaspoon salt and 1 small or ½ large Maggi cube.
2. Add to a large pot and bring to a boil over medium heat. Reduce heat to low and continue to cook for 5 minutes.
3. Add 4 cups water. Cover and cook over high heat, adding more water if needed to cook beef until tender. Mix groundnut paste with remaining 3 cups water. Add and bring to a boil.
4. Add eggplant, garden eggs, onion, pepper, fresh tomatoes, tomato puree and Maggi. Cover and bring to a boil. Continue to cook for 15 to 20 minutes or until all the vegetables are soft.
5. Taste and add more salt if desired. Reduce heat to low and simmer for 10 minutes or until soup is slightly thick.

Serve hot with your favorite boiled tuber, *fufu*, *tuei*, pounded yam, or steamed rice.

CHICKEN GROUNDNUT SOUP

SERVES 6

INGREDIENTS

1 large broiler chicken (2½ to 3 pounds)
Salt, to taste
1 small Maggi cube
1½ cups vegetable oil, for frying
    chicken
2 tablespoons groundnut paste
4 cups water
2 medium eggplants, peeled,
    chopped into small chunks and
    seeds removed.
4 garden eggs, whole or chopped
    into halves
1 medium onion, finely chopped
1 to 3 hot peppers, ground or
    whole (optional)
1 large fresh tomato, chopped
½ cup mushroom, cleaned and
    chopped
1 tablespoon tomato purée

Chicken groundnut soup served with steamed rice and spinach

1. Cut chicken into serving pieces. Remove the skin and discard. Put chicken into a bowl. Season with salt and Maggi.
2. Put chicken into a large pot. Cover, bring to a boil over medium heat and continue to cook until all the liquid around the chicken evaporates. Remove from heat.
3. In a skillet, heat oil over medium and fry the chicken until light brown on all sides. (Use deep fryer to fry chicken, if possible.) Remove chicken and discard leftover oil.
4. Put fried chicken into the large pot. Mix groundnut paste with 4 cups water and add to pot. Bring to a boil over medium heat.
5. Add eggplant, garden eggs, onion, pepper, chopped tomato, mushroom and tomato puree. Cover and continue to cook for 15 to 20 minutes or until all the vegetables are soft.
6. Taste and add more salt if desired. Reduce heat to low and simmer for 10 minutes or until soup is slightly thick.

Serve hot with your favorite boiled tuber, *fufu, tuei,* pounded yam, or steamed rice.

Alternatively, Free-Range Fowl/Game Bird can also be cooked. These birds are however tougher and must be boiled for a longer period. The skins should not be removed and you do not have to fry them. Cook following cooking procedure for *Meat Groundnut Soup* but call the dish after the Free-Range or the particular Game Bird you cook.

PORK GROUNDNUT SOUP: This soup can be cooked using only pork meat, pig's trotters, or a combination of the two meats.

SERVES 6

INGREDIENTS

4 pig's trotters, cut along joints into biting pieces, boiled until tender. Discard stock
½ pound pork meat or other parts of the pork, cooked until tender
2 tablespoons groundnut paste
4 cups water
½ teaspoon salt
1 medium onion, finely chopped or ground
1 to 2 hot peppers, whole or ground (optional)
1 large fresh tomato, finely chopped
1 teaspoon tomato purée
1 small Maggi cube

1. Put pig's trotters and pork meat into a large pot. Then, in a bowl, mix groundnut paste and water to form a smooth liquid and add to pot.
2. Bring the pot to a boil over medium heat. Add salt, onion, pepper, fresh tomatoes, tomato puree and Maggi. Cover and continue to cook for 15 to 20 minutes or until all the vegetables are soft.
3. Taste and add more salt if desired. Reduce heat to low and simmer for 15 minutes or until soup is slightly thick.

Serve hot with your favorite boiled tuber, *fufu, tuei,* pounded yam, or steamed rice.

FISHERMAN'S GROUNDNUT SOUP: Whole fish and/or fish fillet can be used. Fish must be cleaned and properly prepared for cooking. Shrimp and other shellfish can also be used. Dish may be prepared with only one type of seafood or a combination of others, according to preference.

SERVES 6 to 8

INGREDIENTS

4 medium-size fresh, whole
    snapper or tilapia
2 limes
1 small Maggi cube
Salt, to taste
6 to 8 serving pieces of fish
    fillets (optional)
2 tablespoons vegetable
    cooking oil

Fisherman's groundnut soup

3 stems spring onions, chopped (optional)
1 large onion, chopped
3 cloves garlic, chopped
2 tablespoons groundnut paste
4 cups water
1 medium onion, finely chopped
1 to 2 hot peppers, whole or ground (optional)
2 fresh tomatoes, chopped
½ cup mushroom (optional)
1 tablespoon tomato puree
10 large fresh shrimp, cleaned and deveined, seasoned with salt and steamed

1. Clean fish and cut into serving pieces. Rinse and put into a bowl. Squeeze juice from 1 lime and pour over fish. Rub the lime juice all over the fish and then drain off lime juice. Season with salt and Maggi. Put into a large pot and steam over low heat. Remove from heat and keep aside.
2. If including fish fillet, clean using water and 1 lime following the procedure in this recipe for whole fish. Season with salt and fry lightly on each side. Add to fish in the large pot.
3. Then, in a skillet, heat oil over medium heat. Add spring onions, chopped onions, and garlic and sauté until soft and shiny. Remove from heat and add to the pot.
4. Meanwhile, mix groundnut paste with 4 cups water to a smooth liquid. Add to the pot *together* with all the other ingredients *except* the steamed shrimps. Cover and bring to a boil over medium heat.
5. Add shrimp and bring to a boil.
6. Taste and add more salt if desired. Reduce heat and simmer for 5 to 10 minutes or until soup is slightly thick.

Serve hot with your favorite boiled tuber, *fufu, tuei,* pounded yam, or steamed rice.

EGUSI SOUP: This dish, which originated in Nigeria, is now one of the favorite dishes in many countries in the region. In Nigeria, stockfish is often an essential ingredient when cooking *egusi* soup; but in other places like Sierra Leone, it is often cooked without stockfish. *Egusi* is believed to be very rich in protein and carbohydrates.

SERVES 6

INGREDIENTS

¼ cup palm oil
1 medium onion, chopped
2 pounds meat, seasoned with salt and Maggi, boiled until tender.
1 cup smoked fish flakes
2 medium fresh tomatoes, chopped
4 cups water
Salt, to taste
1 small Maggi cube
1 to 2 hot peppers, ground or whole (optional)
1 cup ground *egusi*

1. In a large pot, heat palm oil over medium heat. Add chopped onion and meat and fry for 5 minutes or until onion is soft.
2. Add fish flakes, fresh tomatoes, water, salt, Maggi and pepper. Cover and cook over medium heat for 15 to 20 minutes.
3. Sprinkle with *egusi*. Leave pot open and bring to a boil. (You will see *egusi* curdle like scrambled eggs and the sweet aroma will fill the room.) Taste and add more salt if desired.
4. Reduce heat, cover partially, and simmer for 10 to 15 minutes or until sauce is slightly thick.

Serve hot with your favorite boiled tuber, *fufu*, *tuei*, pounded yam, or steamed rice.

Alternatively, you can cook E*gusi* Soup with any other vegetable oil. Follow the same recipe but replace the palm oil with vegetable oil and add 1 teaspoon tomato puree after adding the *egusi*. The tomato puree will give the soup color.

FRESH FISH PALM OIL SOUP: This is very good with catfish, snapper, or tilapia. Other types of fish are also good with this soup.

SERVES 6

INGREDIENTS

3 medium-size fresh, whole fish, catfish,
    snapper, or tilapia
1 lime
1 plus 1 small Maggi
Salt, to taste
6 baby crabs, cleaned (optional)
1 medium onion, chopped
1 medium eggplant, peeled, chopped into
    small chunks and seeds removed
½ cup palm oil
2 cups water
1 to 2 peppers, ground or whole (optional)

Fresh fish palm oil soup with check rice

1. Clean fish and cut each into 3 to 4 pieces. Wash and put into a bowl. Squeeze juice from lime and pour over fish. Rub the lime juice all over the fish and then drain off lime juice. Season with 1 small Maggi and salt.
2. Put fish into the large pot and steam over low heat for 5 minutes. Add baby crabs and continue to steam for 10 minutes or until both fish and crabs are steamed.
3. Add onion, eggplant, palm oil, water, pepper and Maggi. Cook over medium heat for 15 to 20 minutes or until all the vegetables are soft.
4. Taste and add more salt if desired. Reduce heat and simmer for 10 to 20 minutes or until soup is slightly thick.

Serve with *check* rice, okra rice, or steamed rice.

FISH *BENNISEED*/SESAME SOUP

SERVES 6

INGREDIENT

3 tablespoons *benniseed* paste
3 cups water
All other ingredients in the *Fish Palm Oil Soup* recipe, except the palm oil

Prepare this dish using the *Fish Palm Oil Soup* recipe. Mix the *benniseed* paste with 3 cups water until it is smooth and replace where the original recipe calls for palm oil.

Serve with *fufu* or *tuei*.

Sisterhood Emerging Through Cooking

In West Africa, women cook in different types of kitchens. Some cook in modern kitchens with state-of-the-art equipment. Some cook in makeshift kitchens behind their modest homes. Still others cook in open-yard communal cooking points underneath large trees, as singing birds and crackling monkeys bear witness. The sisterhood among women that is born from cooking in all these varied kitchens is remarkable. Through cooking, women's traditional role of mothering a new generation is given a new meaning. Cooking operates as an age-old means of protecting and defining a cultural identity.

This became very clear for me, many years ago, during a visit to my husband's maternal grandmother. I had a little break from work, so I decided to visit her on my own. I travelled, by road, onboard the only commercial vehicle that was available along the route. The road was rough, and the old Bedford (as it was called) travelled for several hours, stopping at several villages to allow passengers to alight and new ones to board. I arrived at her home in Malelah after about six hours.

A beautiful woman of over seventy years old, Mama Satta Kpagbawai stood six-feet tall in front of her home as she welcomed me with a wide smile. She was the women's leader in the village, and one of the few women who could speak both the Vai and Mende languages. The Massaquois in Sierra Leone were originally members of the Vai and Mende tribes and had always straddled the Sierra Leone-Liberia border. After the Colonial Masters divided the borders, many families were split and those in Sierra Leone integrated into the majority Mende tribe; over time, the Vai language gradually disappeared among them. But there stood my grandmother-in-law, a fountain of knowledge and a physical embodiment of times past. With her arms wide-open, she embraced me and soon proceeded to introduce me to the whole village. Women and men came from all corners of the village to see and welcome me. The experience was moving.

Mama Satta, as she was commonly called, had already prepared a meal of cassava leaves and rice for me and I ate slowly, savoring each mouthful. I enjoyed it thoroughly. The next day, after a breakfast of fresh fish pepper soup and boiled cassava, she prepared to cook the main meal. I quickly volunteered to help, but she refused. Instead, she asked me to sit and watch carefully from a hammock in the backyard where she was cooking. There were coconut and mango trees all around, and the air was fresh and perfumed with nature's ripe fruits. Mama Satta pointed to a mango tree, which stood close to the hammock and abounded with ripe and unripe mangoes, and smiled. She said,

"Help yourself while you watch me cook."

I looked up at the ripe mangoes. The fruit, which hung all over the tree, forced the branches to dangle low, almost above my head. I reached for a medium, smooth, oval-shaped mango. It was as fresh as fresh could be. I washed and peeled it, cutting it, piece by piece, from the seed in the center to its bright orange flesh. As I ate the mango's flesh, layers of its sweet, tangy juice filled my mouth. It was so luscious that I ate in silence. After it was done, Mama Satta and I resumed our conversation while she cooked palm oil soup with fresh fish from the nearby Moa River. "Watch and see," she kept reminding me.

When the soup was ready, she cooked the *check* rice and then served the two separately – the rice in the bigger serving dish and the soup in the medium. She asked me to eat. The food looked good and smelled so wonderful that I wasted no time. I ate greedily. Even today, I can still remember how delicious it was! The flavors were unmatched and the thought of it always leaves my mouth watering. Curiously, as I ate, Mama Satta sat silently and watched me. When I finished, I thanked her for the good meal. She looked directly at me, her eyes smiling deeply into mine, and said, "That's the way my grandson loves it." I smiled back shyly.

To this day, I marvel at the fact that a woman with such vast life experiences and vast knowledge – leadership, languages, music – would choose to pass on a recipe for such a seemingly simple dish. It struck me, when I started writing the palm oil soup recipe, that she did so because it fully captures the many ways that food impacts our cultural identity

Stews and Spicy Fish Dishes

GROUNDNUT STEW: This is one of the first dishes I usually prepare when I invite people for dinner who are not from the region. I have never met anyone who has tasted the West African groundnut soup or stew without wanting to know the recipe. It is perfectly delicious and you too will love it.

MEAT AND OTHER GROUNDNUT STEWS: Various types of meat including beef, goat, chicken, pork, and fish can all be cooked using this recipe. All you have to do is ensure that you use a particular protein item as the main protein ingredient. The soup can then be named after that particular protein ingredient. Therefore, there are beef groundnut stews, chicken groundnut stews, fish groundnut stews, and so on.

SPICY FISH DISHES: Fish is very popular in the region. In a country like Sierra Leone, where the water network is very good, we indulge in a variety of fish dishes, such as spicy fish.

Stews and Spicy Fish Dishes

Groundnut

Chicken Groundnut Stew
Variation: Beef, Pork, or Fish
Goat Meat Light Groundnut Stew
Variation: Beef, Chicken, or Fish

Spicy Stew

Spicy Chicken Stew

Regular Stew

Chicken Regular Stew
Fish Regular Stew
Beef Regular Stew

Palm Oil Stew

Chicken Palm Oil Stew
Fresh Fish Palm Oil Stew
Herring Palm Oil Stew
Other Types of Fish Fillet

Spicy Fish

Spicy Fish Delight
Variations: Fish Fillet

CHICKEN GROUNDNUT STEW: This recipe can be used to cook any kind of meat or fish. Pork meat can also be cooked using this recipe. This recipe can also be used to cook any other domesticated fowl or any game bird. These birds however have to be cooked for a longer period before frying.

SERVES 6

INGREDIENTS

1 large broiler chicken (2½ to 3 pounds)
1 teaspoon salt or to taste
1 small Maggi cube
1 cup oil or enough for frying chicken, plus ½
    cup vegetable oil, for cooking stew
1 large onion, finely chopped
1 medium eggplant, peeled, chopped into
    small chunks and seeds removed
1 to 2 hot peppers, ground or whole (optional)
1 medium fresh tomato, chopped
1 teaspoon tomato purée
1 tablespoon groundnut paste
1½ cups water

Chicken groundnut stew with boiled rice

1. Cut chicken into bite-size pieces, remove the skin and discard. Put chicken into a bowl, season with salt and Maggi, and put into a large pot. Cover and bring to a boil over medium heat and continue to cook until all the liquid around the chicken evaporates. Remove from heat and put aside.
2. Pour oil into a skillet and heat over medium. Fry chicken in batches until light brown on all sides. Remove chicken and discard oil. (Use deep fryer to fry chicken if possible).
3. Return the large pot to medium heat. Add ½ cup vegetable oil and heat for 2 minutes. Add onion and eggplant, fry for 5 minutes or until both ingredients are soft.
4. Add fried chicken, pepper and tomato, stir, cover, and bring to a boil. Add tomato puree, stir, cover and continue to cook.
5. Mix groundnut paste with the 1½ cups water until it is smooth and creamy. Add to the pot, cover and bring to a boil over medium heat. Taste and add more salt if desired.
6. Reduce heat to low and simmer for 5 to 10 minutes or until liquid is a thick gravy.

Serve hot with steamed rice, okra rice, or *crain-crain* rice.

Variation: Beef, Pork, or Fish: Using the recipe above, substitute chicken for beef, pork, or fish. And, as you may have already seen, you can name the groundnut stew after the main protein. For example, when fish is the main protein, the dish should be called "fish groundnut stew"

GOAT MEAT LIGHT GROUNDNUT STEW

SERVES 6

INGREDIENTS

2 pounds goat meat
1 plus 1 small Maggi
Salt to taste
4 cups water or enough to boil meat until tender
4 tablespoons vegetable oil plus 4 tablespoons palm oil
1 large onion, finely chopped
1 medium eggplant, peeled, chopped into small cubes and seeds removed
1 cup smoked fish flakes
½ cup mushroom (optional)
3 cups water
1 tablespoon groundnut paste
1 teaspoon tomato purée
1 to 2 hot peppers, ground or whole (optional)
2 medium tomatoes, chopped

1. Cut goat meat into serving pieces, put into bowl, wash and drain off water. Season with salt and 1 Maggi.
2. Put meat into a large pot and bring to a boil over medium heat. Reduce heat to low and continue to cook for 5 minutes. Add 4 cups water. Cover and cook over high heat, adding more water if needed to cook the meat until it is tender. Continue to cook until most of the liquid evaporates and meat is tender. Remove pot from heat and put aside.
3. In a large pot, add vegetable oil together with the palm oil and heat over medium heat for 2 minutes. Add goat meat onion and eggplant. Cook, stirring occasionally until onion and eggplant are soft. Add fish flakes, mushroom and Maggi. Cover and continue to cook for 10 minutes.
4. Meanwhile, mix groundnut paste with 3 cups water until it is a smooth liquid. Add to pot, cover and bring to a boil. Add tomato purée, pepper, and fresh tomatoes, bring to a boil.
5. Taste, add more salt if desired. Reduce heat and simmer for 5 to 10 minutes or until liquid is slightly thick.

Serve hot with steamed rice, okra rice, or *check* rice.

Variation: Beef, Chicken, or Fish: Using the recipe *for Goat Meat Light Stew,* substitute goat meat for beef, chicken or fish. You can then name the light stew after the main protein. For example, when chicken is the main protein, the dish should be called "chicken light stew".

SPICY CHICKEN STEW

SERVES 6

INGREDIENTS

1 large broiler chicken (2½ to 3 pounds)
1 small Maggi cube
½ teaspoon black pepper
1 teaspoon salt or to taste
1 cup vegetable oil, for frying chicken, plus 3 tablespoons vegetable oil, for cooking stew
3 stems spring onion, chopped into 1-inch strips
1 large onion, finely chopped
2 cloves garlic
3 medium slices pumpkin, peeled or unpeeled (optional)
2 cups water
1 small eggplant, unpeeled, cut into medium cubes and seeds removed
Small quantities of bell peppers in different colors cut across into large pieces
1 to 2 hot peppers, ground or whole (optional)
½ cup peas (optional)
1 teaspoon ground cinnamon

1. Chop chicken into large serving pieces. Remove the skin and discard. Put chicken into a bowl, wash and drain off water. Season with Maggi, black pepper, and salt. Put into a large pot. Cover and bring to a boil over medium heat Continue to cook until liquid around the chicken evaporates. Remove from heat and put aside.
2. In a skillet, heat 1 cup oil over medium heat and fry chicken until light brown on all sides. (Use deep-fryer to fry chicken, if possible.) Remove chicken from skillet and discard oil.
3. In the large pot, heat 3 tablespoons oil over medium heat. Add spring onions, chopped onions, and garlic and fry until soft. Add pumpkin slices and water, and then cook over high heat for 10 minutes. Add chicken and eggplant and then bring to a boil. Add bell peppers, pepper, peas and cinnamon and bring to a boil.

4. Taste and add more salt if desired. Reduce heat to low and simmer for 15 to 20 minutes or until stew is thick.

Serve hot with steamed couscous or steamed millet.

Spicy chicken stew with couscous

CHICKEN REGULAR STEW

SERVES 6

INGREDIENTS

1 large broiler chicken (2½ to 3 pounds)
1 plus 1 small Maggi cube
Salt to taste
1 cup vegetable oil, for frying chicken, plus ½ cup vegetable oil, for cooking stew
1 large onion, finely chopped
2 cloves garlic, chopped
1 large eggplant, peeled and chopped into small chunks and seeds removed
1 to 2 hot peppers ground or whole (optional)
2 teaspoons tomato purée
1 cup water

1. Chop chicken into bite-size pieces, remove skin and discard. Put chicken into a bowl. Wash and drain off water. Season with salt and 1 Maggi. Cover and bring to a boil over medium heat. Reduce heat to low and simmer until most of the water evaporates. Remove from heat and put aside.
2. In a skillet, heat 1 cup oil over medium heat and fry chicken until light brown on all sides. Remove chicken and discard oil.
3. Pour ½ cup oil into a large pot and heat over medium heat. Add onions and garlic and stir together. Add eggplant and fry for 5 minutes or until all ingredients are soft and evenly blended.
4. Add pepper and tomato puree. Stir, and then, add fried chicken, Maggi and 1 cup water. Cover, bring to a boil and cook for 10 minutes.
5. Taste and add more salt if desired. Reduce heat to low and simmer for 10 to 15 minutes or until stew is thick.

Serve hot with *joloff* rice, steamed rice, *check* rice, or your favorite tuber.

Chicken regular stew with check rice

FISH REGULAR STEW

SERVES 6

INGREDIENTS

3 medium-size fresh, whole snapper or tilapia
1 lime
Salt, to taste
2cups vegetable oil for frying fish plus ½ cup vegetable oil for cooking stew.
1 large onion, finely chopped
2 cloves garlic, chopped
1 large eggplant, peeled, chopped into small cubes and seeds removed
1 to 2 hot peppers, ground or whole (optional)
1 small Maggi cube
2 teaspoons tomato purée
1 cup water

1. Clean fish and cut each into 3 to 4 pieces. Put into a bowl, rinse and drain off water. Squeeze juice from lime and pour over fish. Rub the lime juice all over the fish and then drain off lime juice. Season with salt.
2. Pour 2 cups oil into skillet and fry fish in batches. Remove from heat and discard oil. (Use deep fryer if possible).
3. Add ½ cup vegetable oil to a large pot and place over medium heat. Add onion, garlic and eggplant and cook until all ingredients are soft and evenly blended.
4. Add fried fish, pepper, Maggi, tomato purée and water. Cover and cook for 10 minutes.
5. Taste and add more salt if desired. Reduce heat to low and simmer for 10 to 15 minutes or until stew is thick.

Serve hot with *joloff* rice, steamed rice, *check* rice, or your favorite tuber.

BEEF REGULAR STEW

SERVES 6

INGREDIENTS

2 pounds beef
Salt to taste
1 plus 1 small Maggi
4 cups water or enough to boil beef until soft and tender
1 cup vegetable oil
1 large onion, finely chopped
2 cloves garlic, chopped
1 large eggplant, peeled, chopped into small cubes and seeds removed
1 to 2 hot peppers, ground or whole (optional)
2 teaspoons tomato purée
1 cup water

1. Cut beef into serving pieces, wash, drain off water and season with salt and 1 Maggi. Put beef into a large pot and bring to a boil. Reduce heat to medium and continue to cook until most of the liquid evaporates.
2. Add 4 cups water and cook over high heat adding more water if needed. Continue to cook until most of the liquid evaporates and beef is tender. Remove from heat and put aside.
3. In a large pot, heat oil over medium heat. Add beef, onion, garlic and eggplant. Cook, stirring occasionally until eggplant is soft and onion is light brown in color.
4. Add in pepper, tomato purée, water and Maggi. Cover and bring to a boil.
5. Taste, add more salt if desired. Reduce heat to low and simmer for 10 to 15 minutes or until stew is thick

Serve hot with *joloff* rice, steamed rice, *check* rice, or your favorite tuber.

CHICKEN PALM OIL STEW: When cooking this dish, you can use palm oil to fry the chicken and to cook the soup. However, I prefer using other refined vegetable oils (e.g. corn oil, sunflower oil, or groundnut oil) to fry the chicken and palm oil to cook the soup. This applies to all palm oil stews, such as *Fish Palm Oil Stew*

SERVES 6

INGREDIENTS

1 large free-range chicken or game bird (2½ to 3 pounds)
1 small Maggi cube
½ teaspoon salt or to taste
6 cups water
2 cups vegetable oil
1 cup palm oil
1 large onion, finely chopped
1 medium eggplant, peeled, chopped into small cubes and seeds removed
1 cup water
1 to 2 hot peppers, ground or whole (optional)

1. Cut the chicken into serving pieces. (Remove skin only if you prefer to have your free range chicken or game bird skinless). Put chicken into a bowl, rinse with cold water and drain off water. Season with Maggi and salt and put into a large pot. Cover and bring to a boil over high heat. Reduce heat to medium and cook until most of the liquid evaporates.
2. Add 6 cups water. Cover and cook over high heat adding more water if needed to cook the chicken until it is tender. Continue to cook until most of the liquid evaporates and chicken is tender. Remove from heat.
3. Heat vegetable oil in a frying pan. Fry the chicken until light brown on all sides. (Use deep fryer to fry chicken, if possible.) Remove chicken and discard any remaining oil.
4. Pour palm oil into a large pot and warm over medium heat. Add onions and eggplant. Cook for 2 minutes or until eggplant is soft and onion is light brown in color. Add fried chicken, water and pepper. Cover and cook for 10 minutes.
5. Taste, add more salt if desired. Reduce heat to low and simmer for 10 minutes or until soup is slightly thick.

Serve hot with *check* rice, okra rice, or steamed rice. Any steamed vegetable can also be added to the rice.

FRESH FISH PALM OIL STEW

SERVES 6

INGREDIENTS

3 medium-size fresh snapper or tilapia
1 lime
All other ingredients in the *Chicken
     Palm Oil Stew* recipe, except the
     chicken

To prepare this stew, follow the cooking procedure in the *Chicken Palm Oil Stew* recipe. First, clean the fish wash with water, rub lime juice all over fish and drain off the excess lime juice. (See the procedure for cleaning fish in the *Planning and Preparing Ahead* chapter.) Season the fish with salt and then fry.

Fish palm oil stew with steamed rice

HERRING PALM OIL STEW

SERVES 6 to 8

INGREDIENTS

8 medium-sized fresh herring
1 lime
All other ingredients in the *Chicken and Palm Oil recipe,* except the chicken.

To prepare this stew, follow the cooking procedure in the *Chicken Palm Oil Stew* recipe. First, clean the herring by rinsing it in lime and water. (See the procedure for cleaning fish in the *Planning and Preparing Ahead* chapter.) Drain off lime and water. Season the herring with salt and then fry.

OTHER TYPES OF FISH FILLET: Use several pieces of fried fish fillet and follow the cooking procedure in the *Chicken and Palm Oil Stew recipe.*

SPICY FISH DELIGHT

SERVES 3

INGREDIENTS

3 medium-size whole tilapia or snapper, cleaned with scales, fins, tails, and gills removed
1 plus 1 lime,
1 teaspoon salt or to taste
1 small Maggi cube
2 cups vegetable oil, for frying fish, plus 3 tablespoons for sauce
2 stems spring onion, about 5 leaves, chopped into 1-inch strips
1 medium onion, finely chopped
2 cloves garlic, finely chopped
½ cup mushroom, cleaned and washed (optional)
Small quantities of green, yellow, and red bell peppers, finely chopped, to measure 1 cup
2 tablespoon stock or water

1. Rinse fish and pat dry. Place on cutting board and cut 3 diagonal, evenly spaced lines on each side. Wash in cold water, rinse, and drain off the water. Squeeze juice from 1 lime and rub the juice all over the fish. Drain off lime juice.
2. Season fish with salt and Maggi. Place fish into bowl and let it stand for 10 minutes.
3. In a skillet, heat oil over medium heat and deep-fry fish until golden brown on the outside. (Use a deep fryer to fry fish, if possible.)
4. Remove fish and place over absorbent paper to drain off oil. Put onto plate and keep in a warm oven. Discard the oil.
5. In the skillet, heat 3 tablespoons oil over medium heat. Add spring onion and stir for a few seconds. Add onion and garlic and sauté until soft. Add mushroom and fry for 1 minute.
6. Stir in bell peppers and continue to fry for another 1 minute. Stir in the stock or water and bring to a boil.
7. Taste and add more salt if desired. Remove from pot. Spread some of the sauce evenly onto a serving plate.
8. Remove fish from oven and place over the bed of sauce on plate. Pour the remaining sauce over the fish. Slice 1 lime and place over the fish.

Serve hot with fried or boiled tubers, tree crops, or steamed rice.

Variations: Fish Fillet: Using the recipe above, substitute in fish fillet or deboned herring. However, if you use herring, do not add salt – the other seasonings in the recipe contain enough salt. Any additional salt will only make the fish taste extremely salty.

Spicy fish dish (Tilapia Fish)

Spicy fish dish served with fried plantains (Snapper Fish)

Main Dishes: Palaver Sauces, Mixed Sauces, and Plassas

In the region, *palaver* sauces are also referred to as mixed sauces or *plassas*. It is a dish made with vegetables that are combined with protein and other ingredients. *Palaver* means uproar or commotion. The idea of *palaver* (or commotion) is literally understood as an encounter between various protein and vegetable ingredients in one pot; it is often called a dish that contains "all the creatures." People tell stories of the tumult, in a *palaver* sauce, between all the creatures in the dish with each telling the other, "I taste better than you and I am going to prove it." In short, you invite a "commotion" of flavors to your palate when you put all of the various proteins and other ingredients together in one place.

Mixed sauces and *plassas* are often used interchangeably to refer to *palaver* sauces. The reason for the reference to mixed sauce is evident and appropriate, given the varied mix of ingredients. The reference to *plassas*, perhaps, is more nebulous; but in my opinion, it has a far deeper meaning. I find that the word '*plassas*' has an onomatopoeic quality that evokes the idea of the sauce 'plastering' itself and fully enveloping the carbohydrate component of the dish. In my view, *plassas* essentially is the crowning glory that puts a seal over the whole meal by animating the carbohydrate.

Palaver sauces are made by combining proteins, vegetables, and oils to produce a delicious main meal. The protein ingredients, such as meats, fish, or beans, have to be very soft and tender. To reduce cooking time, it is advisable to prepare these ingredients in advance. (See the *Planning and Preparing Ahead* chapter for the cooking procedures.) Palm oil is very popular for cooking mixed sauces; but they can also taste very delicious if other vegetable oils, like coconut, groundnut, corn oil, or any of your favorite cooking oils, are used. *Palaver* sauces are served with staples and other carbohydrate foods.

There are also vegetarian variations of all these sauces. Very often, during the rainy season, when there is a shortage of food, only the vegetables are available in abundance. During these times, people – particularly in the rural areas of Sierra Leone – tend to cook these vegetables without meat or fish. Instead they add more beans, mushrooms, and various types of garden eggs. These variations are provided in some of the recipes in the *Main Dishes: Vegetarian Soups and Sauces* chapter.

Main Dishes: (Mixed Sauces 1)
Cassava Leaf, Potato Leaf, and Others

Cassava Leaf   Cassava Leaf Sauce
                     Variations: Alternative Ingredients

Potato Leaf   Potato Leaf Sauce
                     Variations: Swiss chard, Spinach and More

Greens   Greens Sauce

Food Story   The First Time I Prepared Cassava Leaf Sauce Alone

CASSAVA LEAF SAUCE: This exceptional vegetable is very nutritious and exceedingly popular in West Africa as well as in many other countries outside the region. For many of you who are familiar with cassava leaf sauce (or *sakii tomboi,* the traditional name of the sauce in Sierra Leone), I suspect that this will be the first recipe in this book that you will examine!

The West African cassava leaf recipe calls for the leaf to be finely ground. This vegetable is now available in Asian and other ethnic food stores in the West. Look for the ground cassava leaf that is neatly packaged for export. When you buy the frozen ground cassava leaf, defrost and put it in a blender for a few seconds to ensure that it is finely ground.

The magical and somewhat curious aspect about cassava leaf sauce is that it always tastes better over time. During a mealtime conversation, I expressed this phenomenon to a family friend, who reminded me, very enthusiastically, about a legend from Sierra Leone. As the myth goes, there is a competition and *"palaver"* among the ingredients during the cooking phase. After the sauce has been cooked and preserved overnight, all the ingredients finally realize that they are all inescapably mixed together. As a result, the ingredients thus say to each other, "We are in this together. So let us stop fighting and just do our best to create a great dish." The ingredients all comply. So, after the cassava leaf has finished cooking, the ingredients finally end the antagonism and decide to compliment each other's flavors, and to give the sauce the best taste possible.

You can, therefore, enjoy the sauce immediately after its preparation; or, you can preserve it to serve later without losing the benefits of its delicious flavor. So, do not hesitate to cook more than you need. You can always keep some frozen and eat it when you are ready.

I have never met anyone who, after tasting a properly cooked cassava leaf sauce, did not crave more and ask for a recipe. This is one of the reasons why, as a child, I was determined to learn to cook this dish as soon as I could. (See (*Food Story: The First Time I prepared Cassava Leaf Sauce Alone* in this chapter).

CASSAVA LEAF SAUCE

SERVES 6 to 8

INGREDIENTS

4 cups plus 1 cup water
2 cups or 2 small packets frozen
    cassava leaf, each packet weighing
    8 ounces, finely ground
1 small eggplant, peeled, chopped into
    small chunks and seeds removed
1 tablespoon *ogiri*, crayfish, *kenda*, or
    powdered shrimp
1 cup palm oil
1 tablespoon groundnut paste
2 pounds beef, seasoned with salt and
    Maggi, boiled until tender
½ cup small smoked fish flakes, from herring or bonga (optional)
1 cup large smoked fish flakes, from snapper, tilapia, catfish, or barracuda
1 medium onion, finely chopped, plus 1 small onion
2 young, fresh okra pods, grated, to measure 1 teaspoon
1 to 2 hot peppers, ground or whole (optional
1 small Maggi cube
1 teaspoon salt or to taste

Cassava leaf sauce with check.

1. Add 4 cups water to a large pot. Cover and bring to a boil over high heat. Add ground cassava leaf and eggplant. Cover and continue to cook for 25 minutes or until eggplant is very soft.
2. Add ogiri (or a substitute) and palm oil. Cover and bring to a boil.
3. Mix the groundnut paste with the 1 cup water into a smooth liquid and add to pot. Add beef, small and large fish flakes. Cover and bring to a boil.
4. Add onion, okra, pepper, Maggi and salt. Cover and continue to cook for 15 minutes.
5. Taste and add more salt if desired. Reduce heat to low and simmer for 10 to 20 minutes or until sauce is thick.

Serve hot with steamed rice or *check* rice.

Variations: Alternative Ingredients: This delicious sauce can be cooked with different types of ingredients. I have listed four variations below.

Variation: Cassava Leaf Sauce cooked with chicken: Prepare this dish using the *Cassava Leaf sauce* recipe, but replace the beef with chicken. Chop the chicken into serving pieces, season with salt, boil until tender, and then fry. Add the fried chicken where the original recipe calls for beef.

Variation: Cassava Leaf Sauce cooked with other types of meat: With the exception of pork meat, this delectable sauce can be prepared by replacing the beef with any other meat or poultry. Smoked fish must never be omitted because it adds a special flavor that enhances the taste of the sauce.

Variation: Cassava Leaf Sauce cooked with various other ingredients: In addition to the ingredients for traditional *Cassava Leaf Sauce*, the following can also be added to the cassava leaf as it cooks:

50 grams broad beans, boiled until tender, eyes removed
100 grams baby crabs, steamed

To prepare, follow the cooking procedure in the *Cassava Leaf Sauce* recipe. Add the broad beans and steamed crabs where the original recipe calls for beef.

Variation: Cassava Leaf Sauce cooked with other types of oil: Cassava leaf sauce can be prepared by replacing the palm oil with any other vegetable oil. Coconut oil has a unique, nutty flavor, but other vegetable oils also produce their own memorable tastes. Add the oil of your choice where the original recipe calls for palm oil.

Cassava leaf can also be cooked as a vegetarian sauce. (See the *Main Dishes: Vegetarian Soups and Sauces* chapter.)

POTATO LEAF SAUCE: In Sierra Leone, the traditional name for potato leaf sauce is *jolabetei.* Although there are instances where people cook the leaves of sweet potatoes, these do not taste like the real potato leaves. Actual potato leaves are grown only for their leaves and should not be confused with the leaves from sweet potatoes, which are also edible. When potato leaves are cooked using the *Potato Leaf Sauce recipe,* the end result is a delicious sauce that has its own unique flavor. (Read more about potato leaf in the *Food Story: A Craving for Lost Vegetables* chapter.)

In the absence of potato leaves, Italian spinach is a good substitute. Both vegetables possess high water content and shrink considerably when cooked. If you follow the cooking procedure below, Italian spinach can taste just like potato leaves. Because Italian spinach holds a larger quantity of liquid in their leaves, I normally cover the pot partially while it cooks to allow the liquid to evaporate and dissolve.

POTATO LEAF SAUCE

SERVES 6

INGREDIENTS

3 handfuls potato leaves, washed and finely chopped
2 cups water
½ cup whole smoked, dried shrimp/prawns (optional)
1 cup palm oil
1 tablespoon ground *ogiri*, ground *kenda,* or crayfish powder, for aroma
2 pound beef, boiled until tender, cut into 1-inch serving cubes
6 garden eggs, stalk removed and cut into halves (optional).
½ cup small smoked fish flakes, from herring or bonga
1 cup large smoked fish flakes, from snapper, tilapia, catfish, or barracuda
1 cup broad beans, soft-boiled, eyes removed (optional)
1 medium onion, finely chopped
1 to 2 hot peppers, ground or whole (optional)
1 teaspoon salt or to taste
1 small Maggi cube

Potato leaf sauce

1. Put the potato leaves into a bowl. Add enough cold water to cover and wash gently. Put the leaves into a colander and set aside so that water continues to drain off.
2. Put 2 cups water into a large pot. Wash dried shrimp and add. Bring to a boil over high heat. Add palm oil and *ogiri* (or a substitute) and bring to a boil. Add beef and garden eggs. Cover and cook for 10 minutes.
3. Add small and large fish flakes, beans, onion and pepper. Cover and cook over medium heat for 20 minutes or until most of the liquid evaporates - content should be about to stick to the bottom of the pot and you should see bubbles of oil.
4. Add potato leaves and sprinkle in salt and Maggi. Cover and bring to a boil. Using a wooden spoon, stir gently to ensure that potato leaves are at the bottom or evenly mixed with the other ingredients. Cover and cook over medium heat for 10 minutes.
5. Taste and add more salt if desired. Reduce heat to low and simmer for 10 to 15 minutes or until sauce is thick- - it should smell so good that your mouth waters!

Serve hot with steamed rice or *check* rice.

Variations: Swiss chard, Spinach and More: *Potato Leaf Sauce* can be cooked with alternative vegetables or different types of proteins other than beef. It can also be cooked with groundnut paste as well as other types of oils. I have listed six variations below.

Variation: Swiss chard: Prepare this dish using the *Potato Leaf Sauce* recipe, but replace the potato leaf with Swiss chard.

Variation: Fresh Italian spinach: Follow the same cooking procedure as in the *Potato Leaf Sauce* recipe. However, Italian spinach contains a lot more water than the potato leaf. Therefore, after adding the spinach, keep the pot partially covered so that water will evaporate quickly as the sauce cooks.

Variation: Frozen spinach: Take 2 packets of frozen spinach, defrost, and squeeze out water. Then, follow the same cooking procedure as in the *Potato Leaf Sauce* recipe.

Variation: Potato leaf Sauce or an alternative vegetable with other proteins: *Potato Leaf Sauce* can also be prepared with other meats or chicken. Again, do not use pork. Always add smoked fish to the meat, game, or poultry. Note that when using chicken, for cooking any type of *palaver* sauce, it is better to process and fry the chicken before adding it to the sauce. (See the *Planning and Preparing Ahead* chapter.)

Variation: Potato leaf or an alternative vegetable with groundnut: Using the *Potato Leaf Sauce* recipe, reduce the palm oil to ½ cup and add 2 tablespoons groundnut paste. Mix the groundnut paste with some of the water and add it shortly after adding palm oil. You will have a delicious groundnut paste potato leaf.

Variation: Potato leaf or an alternative vegetable with other types of oil: Replace the palm oil in the *Potato Leaf Sauce* recipe with any other vegetable oil and you will have a potato leaf sauce that has its own memorable lip-smacking flavor.

GREENS SAUCE

SERVES 6 to 8

INGREDIENTS

¼ teaspoon bicarbonate of soda
3 bundles greens, finely chopped
All other ingredients in the *Potato Leaf Sauce* recipe, except the potato leaves

1. Dissolve bicarbonate of soda (or a little bit of salt) in a large bowl of water. Add to greens and using your hand, rub them together. Drain in colander and set aside to drain further.
2. Follow the cooking procedure in the *Potato Leaf Sauce* recipe, but add the greens where the original recipe calls for potato leaf.

Serve with boiled rice.

The First Time I Prepared Cassava Leaf Sauce Alone

While living in Kenya, I invited some guests to our home for dinner. The dishes were labeled by name and it was evident that, out of all of them, the Groundnut Soup was a clear favorite. After all, the concept of groundnut as a main ingredient in a sauce was familiar to all my guests. My foreign guests, however, were entirely unfamiliar with the most distinct dish on my table - Cassava Leaf *Palaver* Sauce, unlike my husband and I, everyone took a small portion of the Cassava Leaf Sauce. However, as the evening progressed, I noticed, with delight, that all of my guests had taken a second serving.

Then one of my guests caught my eye. She said jovially,

"This dish is very good and it seems that we are all enjoying it."

Everybody laughed amicably as they inquired about how the dish was prepared. Before I could answer, another lady asked,

"When and how did you learn to cook it?"

At this stage, the bowl of Cassava Leaf Sauce was empty and everyone was asking for the recipe. I decided that it was a good time to recount a fond memory.

I must have been ten years old. By then, all I knew about cooking had come from watching and helping my mother prepare our meals. However, I felt that I had a good enough understanding of all the meal components – namely, carbohydrates, proteins, and vegetables. I knew how to boil tubers, to debone smoked fish, and to prepare various other protein ingredients. I could also chop vegetables and prepare pepper and onion for cooking. With these skills under my belt, I was desperate to try cooking my favorite meal. So I kept begging my mother to allow me to cook the Cassava Leaf Sauce. At first, she was reluctant. However, she soon relented once she saw how keen I was and, perhaps, because she realized it would be a help to her. Whatever the reason, she decided to give me the chance to try.

I still remember the day very clearly. It was a Saturday. As it was not a school day, it was my usual day for rendering full assistance with the cooking. That day, *yei* – as I fondly called my mother using the Mende word for mother – gave me the chance to cook the dish all by myself. With a basket in my hand, I took the ten minute stroll to our vegetable garden and happily picked some fresh cassava leaves. Once inside, I washed the vegetables and then ground them using a mortar and pestle. A few steps away from me, the large pot, which was balanced on top of three stones and heated by firewood, was already full of water and boiling away.

My mother placed the freshly slaughtered chicken into the boiling water for a few minutes. A male relative had killed the chicken earlier because, as is the tradition among our people, a man always kills the chicken. I watched my mother remove the chicken from the boiling water and place it into a large bowl. Together, we removed the feathers from the chicken and then cleaned and chopped it along its joints into bite-size pieces. Once we were done, my mother left everything in my hands. She departed the house to attend to other pressing matters of the day. I was left to cook the full meal without supervision. I felt grown up and delighted at the confidence my mother had placed in me. I wanted to cook the best Cassava Leaf Sauce possible, but I knew I just had to wait and see.

I cooked by following the steps I had memorized from watching my mother. I seasoned the chicken with salt and boiled it until it was soft. I added ground cassava leaves to the pot of water, cooked it over high heat, and added other ingredients, just as I believed mother had done. There were no specific measurements for the ingredients, so I made estimations for everything – the salt, the pepper, and so on. I assumed that my estimates would be as correct as my mother's were. I finished cooking the Cassava Leaf Sauce and was satisfied. I then prepared the rice until it was nice and fluffy. At about this time, *yei* had returned from the market. I excitedly stirred the Cassava Leaf Sauce once again, with a wooden spoon, and placed the spoon close to my nose to slowly smell the sauce. I could smell the good flavors in the dish, all the way to the back of my throat. I was happy and looked forward to eating my meal as soon as it was done. *Yei* told me the food smelled good. However, she said it in such a way that I felt the food was not as perfect as it could have been. Still, I decided to wait to see what others would say after they had eaten the food.

Yei dished out the meal and soon it was time to eat. She sat with the other adults in front of one big tray. All the children ate from our little individual dishes. Eating in a group from one big tray was the convivial and traditional way many people ate. Everyone was expected to eat from his own section of the tray. Jumping to another section of the plate, in front of another person, was considered rude. I washed my right hand because our culture demanded that one should not eat with one's left hand. I quickly mixed my food with my hand and took a handful helping to my mouth. "This is good!" I thought, as I ate greedily. The adults were watching me, but I paid no attention to them. I was fully absorbed by the dish I had prepared. But then my mother, who had finished eating, spoke to me, and I looked up. First, she reminded me that it was bad manners to hold my forehead with my left hand while eating, as I was doing at the time.

"Don't you see that your fingers cover your view if you place your hand over your forehead while eating?" she asked. I looked up, and she recognized that though I was quiet and attentive, all I wanted to do was to continue eating silently.

Then she quickly explained, "If you can only avoid covering your view while you eat, you can enjoy the privilege of inviting people passing by to share your meal with you."

I smiled a little, but said nothing, as I was not supposed to talk with food in my mouth. This too was considered to be very bad manners. I got the feeling that my mother was delighted at the display of my good manners, even after being provoked to talk while eating. I removed my left hand from my forehead and continued to enjoy my meal, with satisfaction.

At the end of the meal my mother and the other female relatives, with whom she was eating, gave me feedback.

"The cassava leaf was so good that you could not even look up at us when we were looking at you," they all commented together, as if it were rehearsed.

I smiled, but then they quickly added,

"It could have been better if you had fried the chicken before adding." They reminded me that you do not have to fry beef before adding it to cassava leaf, but chicken must always be boiled and then fried. I looked up at them quizzically and they realized that I wanted to know the reason behind this suggestion.

My mother quickly volunteered an answer,

"The cassava leaf will taste better and so will the chicken in the cassava leaf if cooked this way."

I honestly did not feel that my cassava leaf and chicken could have tasted better. This was probably because I was only served a small piece of chicken; the best parts were always given first to the adult males in the household. By the time my mother reached my dish, I had only received a small piece. My mother, however, stated that the chicken fiasco was her fault since she had not allowed me to start frying because of my age. I thanked them all for pointing out my mistake. I also thanked my mother for accepting the blame, but begged her to continue to allow me to cook the dish from time to time. She gave me the green light and I have never stopped cooking cassava leaf, which we fondly refer to as *"sakii tomboi."* As I got older, whenever I had to cook chicken with cassava leaf, my mother always made sure that she fried the chicken for me after I had boiled it.

My guests enjoyed my story and realized the differences in our cultures. Here we were, in another time from different countries, talking and eating, and still enjoying this truly unique dish that I had prepared. Many years ago, I could not have done the same back in my village.

BITTER LEAVES, SORREL LEAVES, AND SORREL FLOWERS: These three vegetables have something in common: they are all usually cooked with *egusi* as part of the ingredient.

Main Dishes: (Mixed Sauces 2)
Bitter Leaf, Sorrel, Spinach, and Others

Bitter Leaf	Bitter Leaf Sauce
	Variations: Regional Differences in Bitter Leaf Sauce
Sorrel	Sorrel Leaf Sauce
	Variation: Sorrel Leaf Sauce without Egusi
	Sorrel Stalk Sauce
	Variation: Sorrel Stalk Sauce without Egusi
Cocoyam Leaf	Cocoyam Leaf Sauce
	Variation: Swiss chard
	Variation: Sierra Leone Alternative
***Gbuhing* (Fiddlehead)**	*Gbuhing* Sauce
***Pillaah*/Collard Green**	*Pillaah* Sauce
	Variation: Collard Green
Food Story	A Craving for Lost Vegetables
Food Story	Far Away and Close at Heart

BITTER LEAF SAUCE: The leaves come from a small evergreen shrub that grows in West Africa. As the name implies, the leaves are bitter; but they are delicious when processed and cooked. This dish is eaten all over West Africa, particularly in Nigeria. It is believed to possess medicinal as well as high nutritional properties. Fresh bitter leaves as well as dried bitter leaves are available in Asian and other ethnic food stores in the West.

The first step in cooking bitter leaf sauce is to remove the bitterness from the leaves. Grinding the fresh leaves, and then washing and rinsing it several times, can achieve this. But, the easiest way is to chop up the leaves into small pieces, put into a pot, and add some bicarbonate of soda. Add water to cover leaves and bring to a boil, leave uncovered, and continue to boil over high heat for 10 minutes. Remove from heat and rinse with cold water. Squeeze water out of the leaves. Mash the leaves with your hands until it looks like they have been ground. It is now ready to cook. This procedure is for fresh bitter leaf only.

Dried bitter leaf is usually sold after most of the bitterness has been removed. Nevertheless, it must be soaked in hot water for 1 to 2 hours to remove the remaining bitterness and to get its freshness out before cooking. For every 5 tablespoon dried bitter leaf you can get 1 cup fresh bitter leaf after soaking, rinsing and draining.

BITTER LEAF SAUCE

SERVES 8

INGREDIENTS

3 pounds assorted meat including beef, oxtail, pig's trotters, goat meat, boiled until tender (you do not have to cook all the types of meat listed, a combination of a few can do)
1 cup palm oil
1 large onion, finely chopped
2 cups water
½ cup dried shrimp (optional)
1 tablespoon *ogiri*, *kenda*, or crayfish powder
1 cup bitter leaf chopped and cleaned (see notes on cleaning bitter leaf above)
¼ cup *bologie* or spinach, finely chopped (optional)
2 cups large smoked fish flakes, from snapper, tilapia, catfish, or barracuda
1 to 2 hot peppers ground whole (optional)
1 small Maggi cube
¾ teaspoon salt
1 cup ground e*gusi*

1. Put assorted meats into a large pot. Add palm oil and chopped onion. Cover and cook over medium heat for 10 minutes or until onion is soft.
2. Add 2 cups water, dried shrimp, and *ogiri* (or a substitute). Cover and bring to a boil.
3. Add bitter leaf and *bologie* (or spinach). Add fish, pepper, Maggi and salt. Cover and bring to a boil. Continue to cook for 10 minutes.
4. Sprinkle *egusi* into the pot. Leave open and bring to a boil. You will see the *egusi* curdle like scrambled eggs. Cover partially and cook for 5 to 10 minutes or until sauce starts to get thick
5. Taste and add more salt if desired. Reduce heat to low and simmer for 10 minutes or until soup has thickened.

Serve hot with steamed *fufu*, *tuei,* or pounded yam.

Variations*: *Regional Differences in Bitter Leaf Sauce: Across the region, this sauce is cooked using slightly different methods, but they often taste very similar. In some instances, spices, like thyme and garlic, can be added. Stockfish and smoked snails are other optional ingredients worth giving a try. If using stockfish, it must be soaked for a few hours to remove some of the salt. Fish must also be properly cleaned before adding it to the pot. In all cases, use an assortment of meat.

When spices are used, they must be added at the same time as the onions. Stockfish can be added at the same time as the steamed shrimp. Add snails along with the assorted meat.

You should be adventurous and cook bitter leaf with as many of the ingredients as possible. The more ingredients you use, the better the end result. Bitter Leaf Sauce is always delicious.

SORREL: Sorrel is believed to have originated in West Africa, but is now grown in many countries around the world. The flowers are dried and used to make beverages. It is popular in the region, particularly in Senegal, where it is referred to as *jus de bissap.* The leaves and the flower stalks are cooked as vegetables.

SORREL LEAVES: These are commonly known as *shakpa* leaves or *satuwi* leaves in Sierra Leone. They have a sour flavor. Before cooking, it must be boiled, washed, rinsed, and then kept in a bowl of cold water. When the sour flavor disappears, it is ready to use for cooking the main dish.

SORREL LEAF SAUCE

SERVES 6 to 8

INGREDIENTS

2 bundles sorrel leaves
All other ingredients in the *Bitter Leaf Sauce* recipe, except the bitter leaves

To prepare this sauce, follow the cooking procedure in the *Bitter Leaf Sauce* recipe, but replace the bitter leaves with sorrel leaves. First, boil the sorrel leaves, wash them in cold water, rinse, and then squeeze the water out.

Variation: ***Sorrel Leaf Sauce without Egusi:*** Sorrel leaves can also be cooked without *egusi*. To prepare this sauce, use the recipe for cooking *Potato Leaf Sauce*, but replace the potato leaves with boiled and drained sorrel leaves and add 2 cups boiled broad beans. (For the *Potato Leaf Sauce* recipe, see chapter on *(Mixed Sauces 1) Cassava Leaves, Potato Leaves, and Others.*)

SORREL STALK SAUCE

SERVES 6 to 8

INGREDIENTS

4 cups sorrel stalk
2 pounds beef, boiled until tender
All other ingredients in the *Bitter Leaf Sauce,* except the assorted meat, bitter leaves and *bologie* or spinach

Sorrel stalks come from sorrel flowers. To prepare this sauce, follow the cooking procedure in the *Bitter Leaf Sauce* recipe, but first, boil the sorrel stalk, wash them in cold water, rinse, and then squeeze the water out.

Serve hot with steamed *fufu, tuei,* or pounded yam.

Variation: ***Sorrel Stalk Sauce without Egusi:*** Sorrel stalk can also be cooked without *egusi*. To prepare this sauce, follow the cooking procedure in the *Potato Leaf Sauce* recipe, but first, boil the sorrel stalk, wash them in cold water, rinse, and then squeeze the water out. Also include 2 cups boiled broad beans.

COCOYAM LEAF SAUCE: This sauce was popular in the rural areas of Sierra Leone many years ago. Like many other sauces, it has disappeared from the Sierra Leone scene. However, it is still a delicacy in Ghana where it is often referred to as *kontomire* stew. Other than pork, this sauce can be cooked using any of the protein ingredients, such as meat, game chicken, or smoked turkey.

COCOYAM LEAF SAUCE

SERVES 6 to 8

INGREDIENTS

Swiss chard cooked as cocoyam leaf sauce served with Fufu. From right, the sauce, Fofo and background foods, center, pepper soup, left, fried plantain, spicy fish dish.

1 cup palm oil
1 medium onion, finely chopped, plus 1
  small onion
2 cloves garlic, chopped
2 pound beef, cut into serving sizes,
  seasoned with salt and Maggi, boiled
  until tender
½ cup small smoked fish flakes, from
  herring or bonga
1½ cups large smoked fish flakes, from
  snapper, tilapia, catfish, or barracuda
2 cups water
1 tablespoon ground *ogiri*, ground *kenda,* or crayfish powder
3 medium fresh tomatoes, finely chopped
½ teaspoon black pepper
2 handfuls *cocoyam* leaves, chopped into medium chunks, washed and drained
1 small Maggi cube
Salt, to taste
1 to 4 hot peppers (optional)
1 cup ground e*gusi*

1. Heat oil over medium heat in a large pot. Add onion and garlic and sauté until soft. Add beef, small and large smoked fish flakes. Add water and *ogiri* (or a substitute) and bring to a boil.
2. Meanwhile, grind small onion and fresh tomatoes and add. Add black pepper, cover and cook for 10 minutes.
3. Add *cocoyam* leaves and bring to a boil. Add Maggi, salt, and pepper. Cook for 20 minutes.
4. Sprinkle *egusi* into pot. Leave open and bring to a boil. You will see the *egusi* curdle like scrambled eggs. Taste and add more salt if desired.
5. Reduce heat to low, cover partially, and simmer for 10 to 20 minutes or until sauce is soft and thick

Serve hot with rice, boiled tuber, *fufu, tuei,* pounded yam, or plantain.

Variation: Swiss chard: In the absence of *cocoyam* leaves, cook Swiss chard by following the recipe for *Kontomire Stew or the cocoyam sauce Sierra Leone variation*

Variation: Sierra Leone Alternative: I remember the Sierra Leone variation of cocoyam leaf sauce very well because it was a popular sauce in parts of Sierra Leone about some 50 years ago. It is slightly different from the *Cocoyam leaf Sauce known in Ghana as Kontomire,* which I cooked and ate in Ghana. For this variation, the ingredients are as follows:

SERVES 6 to 8

INGREDIENTS

1 bundle young cocoyam leaves
2 pound beef, cut into serving sizes, seasoned with salt and Maggi, boiled until tender
2 cups water
1 tablespoon ground *ogiri,* ground *kenda,* or crayfish powder
½ cup broad beans, boiled
1 bundle young pumpkin leaves, finely chopped
1 cup palm oil
½ cup small smoked fish flakes, from herring or bonga
1½ cups large smoked fish flakes, from snapper, tilapia, catfish, or barracuda
1 small Maggi cube
1 to 4 hot peppers (optional)
½ teaspoon salt or to taste

1. Chop cocoyam leaves into medium chunks. Wash and put into a colander and put aside for water to drain off.
2. In a large pot, combine beef and water and bring to a boil over high heat. Add *ogiri* (or a substitute) and broad beans. Bring to a boil.
3. Add cocoyam leave*s and* pumpkin leaves. Cover and bring to a boil.
4. Add palm oil, fish flakes, Maggi, pepper, and salt. Cover and cook for 15 minutes.
5. Taste and add more salt if desired.
6. Reduce heat to low, and simmer for 10 to 20 minutes or until sauce thickens.

Serve hot with steamed rice.

***GBUHING* SAUCE (FIDDLEHEAD):** This vegetable was once well known in Sierra Leone, but appears to have disappeared. I found it in Burlington, Ontario. (See story in the *Food Story: Far Away and Close at Heart*.)

***GBUHING* SAUCE**

SERVES 6 to 8

INGREDIENTS

1 cup *gbuhing* (fiddlehead)
Large bowl of cold water, to clean the *gbuhing*
2 pounds meat, cut into bite-size pieces, seasoned with salt and Maggi, boiled until tender
2 cups water
1 large eggplant or 4 garden eggs from the *pillaah* plant, peeled and chopped into small cubes
1 cup palm oil
1 tablespoon *ogiri*, *kenda*, or crayfish powder, for aroma
1 medium onion, finely chopped, plus 1 small onion, ground
1 cup broad beans, boiled
½ cup small smoked fish flakes, from herring or bonga
1½ cups large smoked fish flakes, from snapper, tilapia, catfish, or barracuda
1 small Maggi cube
1 to 4 hot peppers ground or whole (optional)
½ teaspoon salt or to taste

1. Add *Gbuhing* to a large bowl of cold water. Wash properly to get rid of any mud that may be trapped in the coils.
2. Add to a pot, with enough water to cover by 3 inches, and bring to a boil over medium heat. Continue to cook for 10 minutes to get rid of the bitterness and bad bacteria. Remove from heat and drain off water. Set aside in a bowl of cold water.
3. In a large pot, combine meat and water. Add eggplant (or garden eggs), palm oil, and *ogiri* (or a substitute). Cook for 15 minutes over medium heat. Add *gbuhing*, and ground onion. Cover and bring to a boil.
4. Add onion, beans, fish flakes, Maggi, pepper, and salt. Cover and cook for 10 minutes. Taste and add more salt if desired.
5. Reduce heat to low keep cover on partially and simmer for 5 to 10 minutes or until sauce thickens.

Serve hot with steamed rice.

PILLAAH: The flowers of this green leafy vegetable (see picture in figure XX) grow a special type of garden egg that can be combined with the *pillaah* leaf to prepare the *pillaah* sauce. This vegetable is not as widely available outside of West Africa. However, collard greens, when cooked using the procedures used for cooking *pillaah*, produce a very similar taste.

PILLAAH SAUCE

SERVES 6 to 8

INGREDIENTS

Collard Green cooked as Pillaah

2 bundles *pillaah* leaves
4 cups water
1 medium eggplant or 3 green garden eggs
½ cup dried shrimp (optional)
1 cup okra, chopped into 1- to 2-inch rings
1 cup palm oil
2 tablespoons ground *ogiri,* ground *kenda,*
    or crayfish powder
1 pound meat, cubed and cooked until tender
½ cup small smoked fish flakes, from herring or bonga
1½ cups large smoked fish flakes, from snapper, tilapia, catfish, or barracuda
1 cup broad beans, boiled until tender (optional)
1 to 4 peppers, ground or whole
1 medium onion, finely chopped
1 small Maggi cube
½ teaspoon salt or to taste

1. To clean the p*illaah*, separate the green leaves from the large spine, which is in the middle. Chop each part (leaf and spine) into large chunks and keep separated in two different bowls. Rinse each part and drain.
2. Add 4 cups water to a large pot. Add chopped spine of *pillaah*, eggplant (or garden eggs), and dried shrimp. Cook over medium heat for 10 minute*s.*
3. Add *pillaah* leaves and okra. Bring to a boil. Add palm oil and *ogiri* (or a substitute). Cover and continue to cook for 15 minutes.
4. Add meat, fish flakes, beans, pepper, onion, Maggi, and salt. Cover and continue to cook for 10 minutes. Taste and add more salt if desired.
5. Reduce heat to low and simmer for 5 to 10 minutes or until sauce is thick.

Serve hot with steamed rice.

Variation: Collard Green: In the absence of the *pillaah* vegetable, use collard green to prepare the *pillaah* sauce. Follow the same procedure as in the *Pillaah Sauce* recipe, but replace the *pillaah* with collard green. Also, replace the *pillaah's* garden eggs with eggplant.

Food Story: A Craving for Lost Vegetables

I remember when I was growing up, in the rural part of Sierra Leone, that there were a large variety of vegetables I always craved. As a young adult working in the capital, Freetown, I realized that some of these vegetables were not available in the market. I was disappointed because, back then, I had been taught to believe that these vegetables were very healthy. For me, the inaccessibility of these vegetables was sad on many levels.

We often rightly worry about the loss of one's language because of its potential to endanger the identity of a group of people. However, we should also apply our anxiety to the disappearance of traditional foods because they have the capacity to define our unique identity. They not only nourish us physically, but they sustain, protect, feed, and personalize the people that cook them.

My concern motivated me to start a vegetable kitchen garden where I could grow the traditional vegetables. My garden, on the outskirts of Freetown, was quite big, occupying quite a significant portion of the vast land where my home stood. The garden was so successful that sometimes my friends, who lived downtown in the city, would come up during the weekends to get these vegetables. I planted both the vegetables that were about to disappear and those that were still available in the urban market.

Some of the common vegetables that I planted were cassava leaves, okra, and *crain-crain*. I also planted various vegetables that were at risk of being lost. These included traditional potato leaves, *pillaah*, *paw-paw-daah*, a special type of okra whose dark green leaves are more palatable than the regular okra, cocoyam and pumpkin (for their leaves), and different varieties of garden eggs.

Today, potato leaves are still available in the urban markets, but sometimes it is rare to find the traditional potato leaves. When I was growing up, there were three varieties of potato leaves that were all cultivated solely for their leaves. The potatoes that grew from their roots were too tiny to be edible. Traditional potato leaves have unique names, such as the *"weh-nga-nyi"* variety, which means "very little left over" in Mende. Effectively, it is meant to underscore the fact that this particular variety of potato leaf is so tasty that, when cooked and served with rice, one can eat almost everything no matter how large the serving. There is also the *"kpa-gbay"* variety that means "broom" in Mende. This is supposed to mean that, once served, this potato leaf tastes so good that you will eat all of it to the point of sweeping the plate clean. Then, there is the *"ae-weh-loh"* that means "none left over," which is very much in the same vein as the other names: you can eat everything and have none left over.

These leaves were grown purely for their leaves, and we were told they were very good for the body. Pregnant women were advised to eat boiled rice, every morning, with cooked garden eggs and potato leaves steamed over the rice. These vegetables represented both food and medicine to our people.

Among the 'vanishing vegetables' that I planted was a special variety of okra that was good both for the okra itself and for its broad, dark green leaves. I grew *pillaah* leaves because of their delicious flavor and the variety of edible garden eggs. These types of garden eggs are used to cook vegetables like cassava leaves, p*illaah* leaves, okra leaves, and okra. I also cultivated other varieties of garden eggs. I planted cocoyam and pumpkin mainly for their young leaves, as the cocoa tubers and pumpkin were plentiful in the markets but the leaves were not. In addition, I grew *paw-paw-daah* to use as a spice in my fish dishes. In later years, while travelling around West Africa, I was delighted to find that some of these leaves were still delicacies. In fact, in Ghana, some of these leaves were available in the urban markets. I also found, with pleasure, that in Tanzania, Malawi, and Zimbabwe, people still grow, cook, and eat some varieties of the original potato leaves. The cooking methods are, however, completely different from those in West Africa.

I also tried to cultivate another vegetable called *bologie*, which, to the best of my knowledge, is unique in that it is grown only in Sierra Leone. I have never seen it anywhere else in the region. *Bologie* leaves bring to mind another vegetable I enjoyed as a child that grew in the wild. Mama Yatta, my grandmother, used to love adding it to soups as a seasoning. She called it bush onions; the leaves resembled *bologie* leaves and like the actual plant, it was a creeping plant with triangular, dark green leaves. Unlike bush onions, *bologie* leaves are usually combined with bitter leaves to prepare Bitter Leaf Sauce. In the absence of *bologie* leaves, I usually use chopped spinach as a substitute. Bush onions have disappeared, but I hope the same fate does not befall *bologie* leaves.

During the times that I have lived in the West, I have craved these traditional vegetables; I started to cook the vegetables that were available in the markets to see if they would taste like my traditional vegetables. After many trials, I was delighted to find that there are indeed vegetables that act as useful substitutes and come very close to the original taste. I have realized that Italian spinach, when cooked like potato leaves, can taste like a great traditional potato leaf sauce. I have also found that what is sold in the West as *jute* leaf is actually *crain-crain*. The list below gives full details of the traditional vegetables and the substitutes that are available elsewhere.

Traditional Vegetables	Substitutes available elsewhere
Traditional Potato Leaves	Swiss Chard or Italian Spinach
Cocoyam Leaves	Swiss chard
Pillaah	Collard Green
Okra Leaves	Baby Spinach plus Okra
Mixed Vegetables	Italian Spinach plus Okra
Bologie Leaves	Baby Spinach

My kitchen garden in Freetown disappeared when I moved from my country during the horrible years of war. For me, a good kitchen garden is a source of healthy vegetables. In modern day West Africa, mass urbanization and a lack of adequate research about crops has led to the disappearance of a lot of quality vegetables. To me, there is nothing more satisfying than an opportunity to keep at least some of these vegetables alive.

Far Away and Close at Heart

Growing up, I was privileged to have many "grandmothers." I was fond of all of them, and they all touched my life in different ways. Mama Jattu was one such grandmother. She had the reputation of being the best cook in the village. She was a good woman, and delighted in teaching her many grandchildren how to cook. One of the reasons Mama Jattu and I bonded so well was that I loved to cook. It is interesting that just as I was about to finish the last chapter of this book, something happened that made me feel the presence of my grandmother (who died over forty years ago), as if she were standing right beside me. This is the story:

The doors to the large Metro shop in Burlington, Ontario opened automatically. Walking right through and enthusiastically looking around, my eyes caught sight of the ripe fruits that were colorfully arranged just a short distance from the doors. I noticed that beyond the tempting ripe fruits was a small basket full of familiar vegetables. I moved closer and examined the content. I was thrilled to realize that I was looking at a curly plant that was once part of the Sierra Leonean diet, but had almost disappeared.

I quickly reflected on how Mama Jattu had taught me to cook it when I was a child and how, only a few months before, I had cooked asparagus as a substitute. In my native Mende language, we call it *gbuhing.* It is the curly head of a special fern plant that grows around swamps. Strangely, as I looked at it, I immediately felt the presence of my grandmother. I could even smell the favorite perfume she used to collect from the popular *gbehssay* tree in our village. (*Gbehssay* is a tree that grows wild in eastern Sierra Leone. The back of the tree has a beautiful, unique, and long-lasting fragrance.) It was as if she were standing beside me and telling me, "This is it – this is *gbuhing.*"

I looked at the price tag; it read, "twelve dollars per ounce"! Although expensive, my desire to once again eat it outweighed the monetary consideration. I decided to buy some, but first, I wanted to find out if anybody in the store knew anything about it. The shop staff, in the fruit and vegetable section, knew the name, but that was about it. However, the more I felt the presence of my grandmother beside me, the more I felt obliged not only to buy it but to learn about it from the people who were directly connected with this brand of *gbuhing.*

As I faced the door and held the basket, I continued to smile as I asked everyone who entered the shop about the vegetable. After many trials, without success, a smartly dressed, middle aged, slightly heavyset woman entered and generously returned my smile. She had a happy face and looked very friendly. Then she realized my curiosity.

"You like the fiddlehead, love?" she asked pleasantly.

"Yes, I do. I do very much," I replied. She smiled, and so I asked her more questions, which forced her to stand and continue to talk.

"I am curious about this vegetable and I wish to learn more about it," I told her.

"It is called fiddlehead and it grows mostly along muddy river banks, but it is cultivated commercially in New Brunswick," she replied.

"New Brunswick?" I asked. She nodded, with a smile.

"Oh good, but ...," I began, trying to pose another question. But, before I could finish, she went on to explain that it was a very special delicacy and it was a seasonal vegetable.

"You might as well buy it now because pretty soon, it will not be available," she advised delightfully.

She went on to educate me about its health benefits. According to her, fiddleheads contain antioxidants that help prevent diseases like cancer, cardiovascular disease, and other age-related conditions, like Alzheimer's; they also help to reduce the risk of birth defects. She added that they have a high-fiber content, vitamins A and C, niacin, potassium, phosphorus, iron, and magnesium, and are also low in sodium.

"Buy, and then go home and cook," she told me, with her now familiar smile.

I stood dumbfounded for a while, but then I quickly asked,

"How does it taste and how do you cook it?"

The woman pushed closer to me and explained that the vegetable tastes like a mix of asparagus or green beans with a touch of artichoke. I shook my head as if I could taste what she was describing. Not wanting to waste any more time and concerned that she may prematurely walk away, I asked again, almost immediately,

"How do you cook it?"

She told me to clean the fiddlehead very well. If possible, I should soak it in water to get rid of any mud that may be trapped inside the coils. She added that after properly cleaning the fiddlehead, I should boil it in water, for about ten minutes, to remove the bitterness and bad bacteria. At this stage, I should remove the broken stem, transfer the vegetable to a skillet, sauté it in butter for 5 minutes, and then add lemon and a dash of sea salt.

At this point, I felt my grandmother's presence even more, and this time, it was as if she were reminding me how to cook the vegetable. Her ingredients were an assortment of ingredients that I have outlined in the recipe for the Sierra Leone variation of the Cocoyam Leaf Sauce. Its preparation was similar to the woman's instructions. I knew I had to cook the fiddlehead the way

Mama Jattu had taught me to cook *gbuhing*. As I continued to feel her by my side, I begged her for permission to allow me to use measurements. I felt her nod, and she told me that if I had to use measurements, I should try cooking the dish several times, over and over again, to make sure I maintain the original taste.

The thought mesmerized me so much that I was unaware of exactly when the woman had walked away. When I recovered, I tried to search for her in the shop, but she had vanished – as did the feeling of Mama Jattu standing beside me.

I bought the vegetable, and as I exited the shop, I kept thinking about this incident. The only other time I have ever sensed such a feeling was when I received a very special cookbook as a gift. But, that is another story. I hope to tell it someday.

Gbuhing (Fiddlehead)

Main Dishes: (Mixed Sauces 3) Okra, Crain-Crain, Baby Spinach, Beans, and Others

Main Dishes: (Mixed Sauces 3)

Okra Fried Okra Sauce
Okra Stew
Boiled Okra Sauce
Dried Okra Sauce
Okra-Vegetable Mixed Sauce

Okra Leaf Okra Leaf Sauce
Variation: Okra and Baby Spinach

Crain-Crain *Crain-Crain* Sauce
Variation: Frozen *Jute* Leaf
Variation: Italian Spinach and Okra

Tola *Tola* Sauce

Bor-boueh *Bor-boueh* Sauce

Beans Broad Beans Sauce
Black-Eyed Beans Sauce

Food Story A Vegetable Story from the School Beneath the Ocean

OKRA SAUCE: Okra, also known in many other countries as lady finger or gumbo, is the base ingredient for this sauce. It is slippery and, therefore, provides a thickening effect when cooked on its own or added to soups, stews, and mixed vegetables. It is eaten across the region and in many other parts of the world. There are various ways of cooking okra, including frying or boiling. Dried okra powder can be used to thicken various dishes. When adding fresh okra to soups and stews, leave the okra whole and make light cutting marks along the pods. This way, you can have a thick but non-slippery soup or stew.

FRIED OKRA SAUCE

SERVES 6 to 8

INGREDIENTS

1 cup palm oil
¼ plus ½ teaspoon salt
1 large onion, finely chopped
4 cups fresh okra, finely chopped
1 pound beef, chopped into serving pieces, boiled until tender
2 cups large fish flakes, from snapper, tilapia, catfish, or barracuda
1 to 3 hot peppers, ground or whole (optional)
3 cups water
1 small Maggi cube

1. In a large nonstick pot, heat palm oil over medium heat. Add a pinch of salt and onions. Stir once and then add okra. Spread evenly.
2. Fry, shaking pot occasionally to ensure that okra does not stick to the pot, burn, or break up. Continue to fry for 10 minutes or until onion turns light brown.
3. Sprinkle remaining salt over sauce and then arrange beef in layers on top. Place fish flakes over meat, add pepper, and pour water around the sides. Cover and cook for 10 to 15 minutes.
4. Gently press down the meat with wooden spoon so that it is submerged in the okra sauce. Taste and add more salt if desired.
5. Reduce heat to low and simmer for 15 minutes or until sauce is thick.

Serve hot with rice, *fufu, tuei,* or pounded yam.

OKRA STEW: Prepare this stew using the *Fried Okra Sauce recipe,* but leave okra whole. Trim and cut off the top and bottom of the okra. Make light marks, taking care not to cut too deeply into the okra.

Serve hot with steamed rice, *fufu, tuei,* or pounded yam.

Alternatively, broiler chicken, Free-Range fowl/Game Birds can be used for cooking Fried Okra sauce and also Okra Stew. To cook with broiler chicken, you have to remove the chicken's skin and then season with salt and Maggi. Cook over low heat in its own liquid until all the liquid evaporates. Fry the chicken and then add to the pot where the original recipe calls for beef.

For Free-Range Fowl/Game Bird, there is no need to remove the skin unless you prefer skinless chicken. Just chop chicken into serving pieces, season with salt and Maggi, and then boil in its own liquid until dry. Add water, to cover about 6 inches above the chicken, and boil until tender. Fry and add to sauce where the original recipe calls for beef.

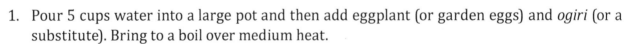

BOILED OKRA SAUCE

SERVES 6 to 8

INGREDIENTS

5 cups water
2 small eggplants or 4 garden eggs, peeled and chopped
    into small chunks
2 tablespoons ground *ogiri,* ground *kenda,* or crayfish
    powder
4 cups fresh okra, finely chopped into 2-inch rings
¾ teaspoon salt or to taste
1 cup palm oil
1 cup boiled broad beans (optional)
1 medium onion, finely chopped
1 to 4 hot peppers, whole or ground (optional)
2 pounds beef, cut into serving pieces, seasoned with salt and Maggi, boiled until tender
1 cup large fish flakes, from snapper, barracuda, catfish, or tilapia
½ cup small fish flakes, from smoked herring or smoked bonga (optional)
1 small Maggi cube

Boiled okra sauce served
with steamed rice

1. Pour 5 cups water into a large pot and then add eggplant (or garden eggs) and *ogiri* (or a substitute). Bring to a boil over medium heat.
2. Add okra and then sprinkle salt over it. Cover and continue to cook for 10 minutes. Add palm oil, beans, onion, and pepper. Cover and bring to a boil.
3. Add beef, fish flakes and Maggi. Cover and cook for another 10 minutes. Gently put a wooden spoon through and taste. Add more salt if desired.
4. Reduce heat to low and cook for 10 to 20 minutes or until sauce is thick.

Serve hot with steamed rice, *fufu, tuei* or pounded yam.

DRIED OKRA SAUCE

SERVES 6 to 8

INGREDIENTS

All the ingredients as in the boiled okra recipe but the boiled beans in this recipe is a must not an option.

DRIED OKRA SAUCE: Prepare this sauce using the *Boiled Okra Sauce* recipe. But, soak the dried okra for 2 hours. Then rinse and cook for a little bit longer than you would cook fresh okra. Add the dried okra at the point where the original recipe calls for okra; but, cook for 20 minutes instead of for 10 minutes. This okra dish comes out nicely if cooked with beans as the additional ingredient. Just add a cup of boiled broad beans when adding the meat.

OKRA-VEGETABLE MIXED SAUCE

SERVES 6 to 8

INGREDIENTS

3 cups water
2 tablespoons ground *ogiri*, ground *kenda*, or crayfish powder
1 cup fresh okra, finely chopped
1 cup palm oil
3 bundles any green vegetable, like potato leaves, Italian spinach, greens, finely chopped
1 pound goat meat or beef, boiled until tender
2 cups large fish flakes, from snapper, tilapia, catfish, or barracuda
1 cup small fish flakes, from smoked herring or smoked bonga (optional)
1 medium onion, finely chopped
1 to 3 hot peppers, whole or ground (optional)
½ teaspoon salt or to taste
1 Maggi cube (optional)

1. Put 3 cups water into a pot. Add *ogiri* (or a substitute) and bring to *a bo*il over high heat.
2. Add okra and then reduce heat to medium. Continue to cook for 10 minutes.
3. Add palm oil and bring to a boil. Add green vegetables and bring to a boil.
4. Add goat meat or beef, fish flakes, onion, pepper, salt, and Maggi. Cover and cook for 15 minutes. Stir gently with wooden spoon so that okra and green vegetables are evenly mixed. Taste and add more salt if desired.
5. Reduce heat to low and simmer for 15 to 20 minutes or until sauce is thick.

Serve hot with steamed rice.

OKRA LEAF SAUCE: The broad okra leaf is used to cook this sauce. The leaf is dark green and is shaped like a maple leaf. In the absence of okra leaves, combine baby spinach with chopped okra, which will give you the same effect as Okra Leaf Sauce.

In the rural parts of Sierra Leone, there was – and still is in some areas – a custom where Okra Leaf Sauce would be prepared by one's mother and/or mother-in-law after delivering a baby. Prior to the delivery, there would be months of preparation to cook this dish. Special types of fish, baby catfish, and different types of small fish would all be smoked. Game meat would also be smoked and preserved. The dish would be prepared on the day of the baby's birth. It was believed that eating this sauce would promote lactation in the new mother. This dish was thus called Nursing Mother's Okra Leaf Sauce.

The sauce was cooked using the following *Okra Leaf Sauce* recipe, although different types of smoked fish were added to Nursing Mother's Okra Leaf Sauce. All the smoked fish had to be boiled and deboned, and then the flaked fish would be added to the sauce. The smoked meat would also be boiled, until tender, before adding it to the cooking sauce.

OKRA LEAF SAUCE

SERVES 6 to 8

INGREDIENTS

3 handfuls okra leaves
3 cups water
1 cup fresh okra, chopped
1 medium eggplant or 4 garden eggs from the *pillaah* plant, peeled, chopped into small chunks
    and seeds removed.
1 cup palm oil
2 tablespoon ground *ogiri,* ground *kenda,* or crayfish powder
1 pound meat, chopped into serving cubes and cooked until tender (use any type of meat except pork)
1 cup large fish flakes, from snapper, tilapia, catfish, or barracuda
½ cup small fish flakes, from smoked herring or smoked bonga (optional)
1 medium onion, finely chopped (optional)
½ teaspoon salt
1 small Maggi (optional)
1 to 2 peppers, ground or whole (optional)

1. Place okra leaves in colander and rinse. To avoid making the leaves slippery, do not rub as you rinse. Chop okra leaves into large chunks and set aside.
2. Put 3 cups water into a pot and add okra. Cover and bring to a boil over high heat. Add okra leaves and eggplant (or garden eggs) and then bring to a boil. Add palm oil and *ogiri* (or a substitute). Cook for 10 minutes.
3. Add meat, fish flakes, onion, salt, Maggi and pepper. Cover and cook over medium heat for 20 minutes. Taste and add more salt if desired.
4. Reduce heat to low and simmer for 10 to 15 minutes or until sauce is thick

Serve hot with steamed rice, *fufu, tuei* or pounded yam.

Variation: Okra and Baby Spinach: In the absence of okra leaf, use okra and baby spinach. Prepare using the recipe below.

OKRA AND BABY SPINACH

SERVES 6 to 8

INGREDIENTS

4 bundles or 4 handfuls baby spinach
3 cups water
1 cup fresh okra, finely chopped
1 medium eggplant or green garden egg, chopped into small chunks
1 cup palm oil
2 tablespoon ground *ogiri*, ground *kenda,* or crayfish powder
1 pound meat, chopped into serving cubes and cooked until tender (use any type of meat except pork)
1 cup large fish flakes, from snapper, tilapia, catfish, or barracuda
½ cup small fish flakes, from smoked herring or smoked bonga (optional)
1 medium onion, finely chopped (optional)
½ teaspoon salt
1 small Maggi cube
1 to 2 peppers, ground or whole (optional)

1. Wash baby spinach and then drain in colander. Do not chop the leaves.
2. Put 3 cups water into a large pot and add okra and eggplant (or garden egg). Cover and bring to a boil over medium heat. Add baby spinach leaves and bring to a boil.
3. Add palm oil and *ogiri* (or a substitute) and then cook for 10 minutes. Add meat, fish flakes, onion, salt, Maggi and pepper. Cover and cook for 15 minutes.
4. Taste and add more salt if desired. Reduce heat to low and simmer for 10 to 15 minutes or until sauce is thick.

Serve hot with steamed rice, *fufu*, or pounded yam.

Baby Spinach plus okra cooked as okra leaf

CRAIN-CRAIN SAUCE: The *crain-crain* vegetable, which is the main ingredient for this sauce, is found in many parts of the world. The slippery, green leafy vegetable is known as *crain-crain* in West Africa, *muranda* in Kenya (East Africa), *molokhia* in Egypt, and *jute* leaves in Asia. In other parts of the world, it is called bush okra or *jew's mallow*, among other names.

In the Western world, it is commonly marketed under the name *jute* leaf. Not only is it available in Asian and other ethnic food stores, but also it can be found sometimes in supermarkets in its frozen form. Where the vegetable is not available, a combination of chopped Italian spinach and chopped okra can do the trick.

It is a delicacy in West Africa and we strongly believe it originated from our part of the world. We use it to prepare *Crain-Crain* Mixed Sauce and in the popular *check* rice.

CRAIN-CRAIN SAUCE

SERVES 6 to 8

INGREDIENTS

3 cups water
4 bundles *crain-crain,* finely chopped
1 cup palm oil
1 tablespoon ground *ogiri* or ground kenda or crayfish powder
1 medium onion, finely chopped
1 pound meat, chopped into serving pieces, boiled until tender (use any type of meat except pork)
½ cup small smoked fish flakes, from herring or bonga
1½ cups large smoked fish flakes, from snapper, tilapia, catfish, or barracuda
1 small Maggi cube
½ teaspoon salt
1 to 2 hot peppers, whole or ground with small onion (optional)

1. In a large pot, bring water to a boil over high heat. Add the *crain-crain.* Cover partially and bring to a boil. Continue to cook for 5 minutes.
2. Add palm oil, *ogiri* (or a substitute), and bring to a boil. Add onion, meat, fish flakes, Maggi, salt and pepper. Bring to a boil and continue to cook for 20 minutes. Taste and add more salt if desired.
3. Reduce heat to low and simmer for 15 minutes or until sauce is thick.

Serve hot with steamed rice, *fufu,* tuei or pounded yam.

Variation: Frozen Jute Leaf: In the absence of fresh *crain-crain* leaves, use frozen *jute* leaves. To prepare, follow the recipe below. Frozen jute leaves are sold either chopped or whole. You can chop the whole frozen leaves before cooking or you can cook it whole.

SERVES 6 to 8

INGREDIENTS

3 packets frozen *jute* leaves, chopped or whole
All other ingredients in the *Crain-Crain Sauce* recipe, except the *crain-crain* leaves

1. Thaw the *jute* leaves until soft enough for a knife to cut through. On a cutting board, cut into small bits with a knife and then allow the leaves to defrost completely. (*Jute* leaves can also be cooked whole. If you choose this option, then do not chop leaves.)
2. Put liquid into pot. Add palm oil, ogiri or substitute and bring to a boil. Add meat and fish flakes, onion and pepper. Cover partially and cook for 10 minutes or until most of the liquid evaporates.
3. Add defrosted *jute* leaves and bring to a boil. Reduce heat to low and continue to cook for 5 minutes. Taste and add more salt if desired.
4. Continue to simmer for 5 more minutes or until consistency is thick.

Serve hot with steamed rice, *fufu,* or pounded yam.

Variation: Italian Spinach and Okra: In the absence of fresh *crain-crain* leaves or *jute* leaves, use a mix of Italian spinach and okra. To prepare, follow the recipe below:

ITALIAN SPINACH AND OKRA

SERVES 6 to 8

INGREDIENTS

2 bundles fresh Italian spinach, finely chopped
1½ cups okra, finely chopped
All other ingredients in the *Crain-Crain Sauce* recipe,
    except the *crain-crain* leaves

Crain-Crain Sauce

1. Add liquid to a large pot. Add *ogiri* (or a substitute) and bring to a boil over medium heat. Add okra. Cover and continue to cook for 10 minutes.
2. Add palm oil and bring to a boil. Add onion, meat, fish flakes and pepper. Cover and cook for another 10 minutes.
3. Add spinach, Maggi and salt. Cover and bring to a boil. Taste and add more salt if desired.
4. Reduce heat to low and simmer for 15 minutes or until sauce is thick.

Serve with steamed rice, *fufu* or pounded yam.

TOLA SAUCE: *Tola,* also known as *kpei* in some parts of Sierra Leone, is the fruit of a type of bush mango seed. It is the base ingredient for *tola* sauce. To cook this sauce, the dry seeds must be finely ground into a smooth powder. Not only is it available in markets in the region, but it can also be found in Asian and other ethnic food stores in other countries. When cooked, it has the appearance of curry stew, but with its own unique, nutty taste.

TOLA SAUCE

SERVES 6 to 8

INGREDIENTS

2 pounds meat, chopped into serving cubes, cooked until tender (use any type of meat except pork)
2 cups large fish flakes, from snapper, tilapia, catfish, or barracuda
1 cup small fish flakes, from smoked herring or bonga
3 cups water
4 tablespoons plus 1 cup palm oil
2 tablespoons ground *ogiri,* ground *kenda,* or crayfish powder
¾ teaspoon salt
1 to 3 hot peppers, ground or whole (optional)
1 medium onion, ground
1 small Maggi cube
3 tablespoons ground *tola*

1. Add meat, fish flakes, and water to a pot. Cover, bring to a boil over high heat and then, add 4 tablespoons palm oil and *ogiri* (or a substitute) and bring to a boil.
2. Add salt, pepper, onion and Maggi. Cover and cook for 20 minutes. Remove from heat and put content into a large bowl. Separate, keeping the hot stock in one bowl and the rest of the ingredients in another.
3. Pour 1 cup palm oil into the pot and heat over medium heat for 5 seconds. Sprinkle the *tola* over the oil stirring continuously at the same time until all the *tola* is added to the pot and dissolved with the oil.
4. Pour in the hot stock as you continue to stir until both the *tola* and stock are evenly mixed. Add the rest of the ingredients and bring to a boil. Taste and add more salt if desired.
5. Reduce heat to low, cover partially and simmer for 5 to 10 minutes or until sauce is thick.

Serve hot with steamed rice, *fufu*, and pounded yam.

BOR-BOUEH SAUCE: *Bor-boueh*, also known as *ogbornor* in other parts of West Africa, including Nigeria, is the base ingredient for this sauce. It is another ty*pe* of bush mango seed. To cook, the dry *seeds* must be finely ground into a smooth powder. Not only is it available in markets in the region, but it can also be found in Asian and other ethnic food stores in other countries.

When ground and cooked, *bor-boueh* has the appearance of curry stew but the smell of spiced fruits.

SERVES 6 to 8

INGREDIENTS

3 tablespoons *bor-boueh*, ground
All the ingredients in the **TOLA SAUCE** recipe, except the *tola*

1. Add meat, fish flakes, and water to a large pot and bring to a boil over medium heat.
2. Add palm oil, ogiri or substitute and cook for 10 minutes. Add salt, pepper, onion and Maggi. Cover and cook for another 10 minutes. Taste and add more salt if desired.
3. Sprinkle *bor-boueh* into pot as you stir. Cover partially and bring to a boil.
4. Reduce heat to low, and simmer for 10 to 20 minutes or until sauce appears thick and about to stick to the bottom of the pot.

Serve hot with *fufu*, *tuei*, pounded yam, cassava, or rice.

BROAD BEANS SAUCE: This dish is considered to be very healthy likely because of its high content of beans. The traditional name for this dish in Sierra Leone is *"Torworgbortoh."*

SERVES 6 to 8

INGREDIENTS

3 cups water
2 small eggplants or 1 large garden egg, peeled, chopped into small chunks, seeds removed.
3 cups broad beans, boiled until very tender
2 tablespoon ground *ogiri,* ground *kenda,* or crayfish powder
½ teaspoon salt
1 cup palm oil
½ pound meat, cooked until tender (use any kind of meat but except pork)
1 cup large smoked fish flakes, from snapper, tilapia, catfish, or barracuda
½ cup small fish flakes, from herring or bonga (optional)
1 to 4 hot peppers (optional)
1 medium onion, ground with pepper
1 small Maggi

1. Put water, eggplant (or garden egg), beans, and *ogiri* (or a substitute) into a large pot. Cover and bring to a boil over medium heat. Then, add salt and palm oil and bring to a boil.
2. Add meat, fish flakes, pepper, onion, and Maggi. Cover and cook for 10 minutes.
3. Reduce heat to low and steam for 10 to 20 minutes or until sauce is thick and about to stick to the bottom of the pot.

Serve hot with rice.

BLACK-EYED BEANS SAU*CE*

*SE*RVES 6 to 8

INGREDIENT*S*

1 cup palm oil
1 medium onion, finely chopped
1 cup large fish flakes, from, snapper, tilapia, catfish, or barracuda
½ cup small fish flakes, from herring or bonga
1 small Maggi cube
½ teaspoon salt
1 to 2 hot peppers, ground or whole (optional)
2 cups black-eyed beans boiled until very tender and almost pulp like

1. Pour oil into a pot and heat over medium heat. Add onion and fry until soft.
2. Add fish flakes, Maggi, salt, and pepper. Cover and cook for 5 minutes.
3. Then add beans along with its stock and cook for 10 minutes. Taste and add more salt if desired.
4. Reduce heat to low and simmer for 5 to 10 minutes or until sauce is thick and about to stick to the bottom of the pot.

Serve hot with boiled or fried plantains, boiled cassava, or boiled yam.

Black-eyed beans served with small chunks boiled cassava

Food Story: A Vegetable Story from the School beneath the Ocean

When my late father-in-law was about seventy years old, he told me a story about an incident at Morbay School, a school that today lies buried beneath the Atlantic Ocean, not far from present-day Bonthe Island in Sierra Leone. The story involved the school's boarding master, a Catholic priest, and his distaste for how the school's cook prepared potato leaves. I know the story to be true because Papa – as we all called him – told it to me, and he had attended Morbay during his youth in the late 1800's.

He told me the story as he praised a potato leaf meal he had just eaten. It still resonates for me because very often food discussions can unveil interesting and hidden stories. It is amazing the number of fascinating things we learn every day around mealtime. Sometimes the information is trivial, sometimes it is vital. But that day, I learned an important piece of history that I have yet to find recorded in any book; a piece of history that happened so many years ago and never caught the eyes of the larger world. Because there was no Internet and no television, stories like his never really travelled far.

As the story goes, a Catholic priest at Morbay School, concerned about the nutrition of the students, tried to convince the African cook that he should prepare potato leaves in a different way.

Now, this was a school where the boys were very happy: they received a first-class education, and had the school survived, some were even planning to train as catholic priests. Fish was in abundance, and the boys went fishing every day for their food. There were a wide variety of traditional vegetables available in the area. The cook was good, and the boys all enjoyed their food.

On this particular day, however, the priest walked towards the cook, who had just chopped the potato leaves and was about to rinse them, and asked one of the nearby students to translate what he was about to say. He told the boy to tell the cook that the potato leaves were always overcooked and, therefore, all the vitamins were being destroyed. He advised the cook to steam the vegetables separately and serve it to the boys with stewed fish. The boy told the cook what the priest had said and the cook smiled. He stood up, smiled at the priest, and then turned to the boy.

In a modest yet pleading voice, he told the boy that potato leaves are best when cooked using his method. The boy reported back to the priest who then asked the cook why he thought so. The cook turned to the boy and replied,

"Tell Father..." He paused and then stopped.

The priest, sensing the cook's hesitation, asked, "Tell Father what?"

Very modestly the cook said, "Tell him that if he comes here to show me how to bake a cake, I will listen because I know it is food from his country. However, we have always cooked potato leaves here and so we know how to cook it best."

The boy told the priest what he had been told. The priest found it funny but pleasing, and he added,

"I think he is right." The boy told the cook and they all laughed.

At the time, I had not started to experiment with cooking spinach as potato leaves. It took years of trying to cook spinach as potato leaves to realize that the priest was, in fact, thinking of spinach when he made his suggestion; although both vegetables contain a lot of water, spinach holds more water in its leaves than potato leaves do. Papa continued by recounting how his school got buried underneath the Atlantic Ocean.

During the holiday, Papa went home to Sulima, another town in the south of the country located near the Atlantic Ocean. One day, everyone went to work inland on the farms; when they returned, in the evening, they found that the town was gone. Something mysterious and disturbing had happened. All the houses had disappeared, and pieces of homes and other buildings were floating in the sea. There was only debris everywhere. They did not know what to call it. The villages around Sulima were informed, and they came to comfort and help their neighbors. Later, they helped them to rebuild their homes.

At the end of the holiday, Papa returned to school. He found that it had been buried underneath the Atlantic Ocean. He learned from the people of Bonthe that a great wave had come and buried the school. "*Kasilla*" – as they called the mysterious goddess of the sea – had claimed Morbay. They believed she was envious of the school, the students, and the Catholic priests who had lived there.

The story about the Morbay cook captures the culinary interactions across cultures that have taken place in West Africa for centuries. Despite everything, West Africans seem to have maintained their traditional foods. Even as old vegetables disappear, it is important that we guard the traditional methods of preparing our dishes.

Over the centuries, culinary exchanges between West Africa and other countries have flourished. Rice, groundnuts, black-eyed beans, okra, and many other crops are known to have arrived in the U.S. and other parts of the world from West Africa. Equally, some variations of chili, tomatoes, green beans, and several other crops and spices have arrived in West Africa from the U.S. and elsewhere. West Africans have incorporated some of these chilies and spices in the preparation of traditional foods. Though they have embraced many of these non-African crops, they have also managed to maintain the same cooking methods learned through example over the ages. Other types of crops from the U.S. and elsewhere, such as lettuce and cabbage, have been used to make salads or cooked to serve with some traditional dishes. Today, it is therefore common to find a traditional *joloff* rice dish served with steamed vegetables and/or salad.

Main Dishes: Vegetarian Soups and Sauces

Vegetarian dishes are often eaten in the region, out of necessity. During the rainy season, for instance, there are plenty of vegetables, while meats, fish, and poultry are harder to come by. During this period, people tend to cook what is available. Mixed sauces are thus prepared using only vegetables; and beans, eggplants, garden eggs, and mushrooms are used in abundance.

Main Dishes: Vegetarian Soups and Sauces

Veggie Soup   Groundnut Veggie Soup
Egusi Veggie Soup
Benniseed Veggie Soup

Veggie Sauce   Cassava Leaf Veggie Sauce
Potato Leaf Veggie Sauce
Variation: Potato Leaf with Groundnut
Italian Spinach Veggie Sauce
Variation: Frozen Spinach
Variation: Spinach with Groundnut
Greens Veggie Sauce
Pemahuin
Variation: Italian Spinach
Pillaah Veggie Sauce
Variation: Collard Green
Black-eyed Beans Veggie Sauce
Variation: Black-eyed Beans with Other Oils
Okra Veggie Sauce
Garden Eggs Delight
Variation: *Garden Eggs* with Other Oils

GROUNDNUT VEGGIE SOUP

SERVES 6 to 8

INGREDIENTS

2 tablespoons vegetable oil
1 large onion finely chopped
2 small or 1 medium eggplants, peeled, chopped into small chunks and seeds removed
1 cup mushroom, washed and chopped into large chunks (Use any edible mushroom)
2 medium fresh tomatoes, chopped
1 medium bell pepper, chopped
2 cups water
2 tablespoons groundnut paste
1 tablespoon tomato paste
1 to 2 hot peppers, chopped or whole (optional)
½ teaspoon salt
1 small Maggi

1. Put oil into a large pot and heat over medium for 1 minute. Add onion and eggplant. Stir and fry for 5 seconds. Stir in mushroom, tomatoes, and bell pepper. Cover, reduce heat to low.
2. Meanwhile, mix water with the groundnut paste and the tomato paste until you get a smooth flowing liquid. Add, cover and cook over medium heat for 10 minutes.
3. Add onion, pepper, salt, and Maggi and then bring to a boil. Taste and add more salt if desired.
4. Reduce heat to low and simmer for 5 to 10 minutes or until soup is slightly thick.

Serve hot with steamed rice, okra rice, *check* rice, *fufu*, or your favorite boiled tuber.

EGUSI VEGGIE SOUP

SERVES 6 to 8

INGREDIENTS

3 tablespoons ground *egusi*
All other ingredients in the Groundnut Veggie Soup recipe, except the groundnut paste

1. Put oil into a large pot and heat over medium for 1 minute. Add onion and eggplant. Stir and fry for 5 seconds. Add mushroom, tomatoes, bell pepper, salt and Maggi. Cover and bring to a boil. Taste and add more salt if needed.
2. Sprinkle ground *egusi* over content in the pot. Do not mix. Leave pot open and bring to a boil. *Egusi* will start to curdle like scrambled eggs.
3. Reduce heat to low, cover partially, and simmer for 10 to 20 minutes or until the soup is slightly thick.

Serve hot with steamed rice, okra rice, *check* rice, *fufu*, or your favorite boiled tuber.

***BENNISEED* VEGGIE SOUP**

SERVES 6

INGREDIENTS

4 tablespoons ground *benniseed*
All other ingredients in the *Groundnut Veggie Soup* recipe, except the groundnut paste

Prepare using the *Groundnut Veggie Soup* recipe, but replace the groundnut paste with ground *benniseed.*

CASSAVA LEAF VEGGIE SAUCE

SERVES 6 to 8

INGREDIENTS

4 cups plus 2 cups water
2 cups or 4 packets cassava leaf, finely ground
1 large eggplant, peeled and finely chopped
1 cup broad beans, boiled until tender
1 cup palm oil
2 tablespoons groundnut paste
1 medium onion, finely chopped
3 fresh okra pods, finely grated, to measure 1 tablespoon
1 to 2 hot peppers, ground or whole (optional)
1 small Maggi cube
1 teaspoon salt or to taste

1. Add 4 cups water to a large pot. Cover and bring to a boil over medium heat. Add cassava leaf and eggplant. Cover and continue to cook for 25 minutes. Then, add beans and palm oil. Cover and continue to cook.
2. Meanwhile, add remaining 1 cup liquid to groundnut paste. Mix together into a smooth liquid and add. Cook for 10 minutes.
3. Add onion okra and pepper. Cover and continue to cook for 15 minutes. Add Maggi and salt. Cook for 10 minutes. Taste and add more salt if desired.
4. Reduce heat to low and simmer for 5 to 10 minutes or until sauce is thick and about to stick to the bottom of the pot.

Serve hot with steamed rice, okra rice, or *check* rice.

POTATO LEAF VEGGIE SAUCE

SERVES 6 to 8

INGREDIENTS

3 bundles potato leaves, washed and finely chopped
1 cup cold water
10 garden eggs
1 cup palm oil
1 cup broad beans, cooked until tender
1 medium onion, finely chopped
¾ teaspoon salt
1 small Maggi (optional)
1 to 2 hot peppers, ground or whole (optional)

1. Wash chopped potato leaves, Put into colander, and put aside so that water continues to drain off.
2. Put 1 cup water into a pot. Add garden eggs. Cover and cook over medium heat until most of the water evaporates. Then, add potato leaves. Cover and bring to a boil.
3. Add palm oil and bring to a boil. Add beans, onion, salt, Maggi and pepper and cook for 10 minutes. Taste and add more salt if desired.
4. Reduce heat to low and simmer for 10 to 20 minutes or until sauce is thick and is about to stick to the bottom of the pot.

Serve hot with steamed rice, okra rice, or *check* rice.

Variation: Potato Leaf with Groundnut: Using the same recipe as *Potato Leaf Veggie Sauce*, reduce palm oil to ½ cup and add 2 tablespoons groundnut paste. Mix the groundnut paste with a little bit of water and add to the pot, after adding palm oil.

ITALIAN SPINACH VEGGIE SAUCE

SERVES 6 to 8

INGREDIENTS

2 cups water
1 cup palm oil
6 garden eggs remove stalk and cut into halves.
2 cups broad beans, boiled until tender
1 medium onion, finely chopped
3 bundles fresh Italian spinach, washed and finely chopped
1 teaspoon salt or to taste
1 small Maggi (optional)
1 to 2 hot peppers ground or whole (optional)

1. Put 2 cups water into a large pot. Add palm oil and garden eggs. Cover and cook over medium heat for 15 minutes.
2. Add beans and onion. Cover and cook for 10 minutes or until water evaporates and content is about to stick to the bottom of the pot.
3. Add chopped spinach, salt, Maggi and pepper. Bring to a boil. Mix gently with wooden spoon to get spinach to the bottom of the other ingredients. Taste and add more salt if desired.
4. Reduce heat to low, cover partially and steam for 5 minutes or until sauce is thick and about to stick to the bottom of the pot.

Serve hot with steamed rice or *crain-crain* rice.

V*ariation: Frozen Spinach:* Frozen spinach can also be used to cook this dish. Take 2 packets frozen spinach, defrost, and squeeze out water. Do not steam, but add spinach where the *Italian Spinach Veggie Sauce recipe* calls for chopped spinach. Use the squeezed water, from the frozen spinach, as part of the 2 cups water from the original recipe for *Italian Spinach Veggie sauce*

Variation: Spinach with Groundnut: Using the same recipe as *Italian Spinach Veggie Sauce*, reduce palm oil to ½ cup and add 2 tablespoons groundnut paste. Mix the groundnut paste with a little bit of water and add to the pot, after adding palm oil.

GREENS VEGGIE SAUCE: To prepare this sauce, follow the cooking procedure in the *Potato Leaf Veggie Sauce recipe*, but replace the potato leaves with greens.

Some Veggie sauces. From left, potato leave veggie sauce, garden eggs delight, okra veggie sauce

PEMAHUIN *(vegetables steamed over cooking rice)* popular dishes that people eat all the time, even during periods when there is no shortage of meat, fish, or poultry. It is believed that this dish has medicinal value, and in the rural south and east of Sierra Leone, it is highly recommended as a regular meal for pregnant women.

SERVES 4

INGREDIENTS

2 handfuls potato leaves, chopped into
    large chunks
2 cups water
6 to 10 garden eggs
2 cups rice
2 tablespoons ground *ogiri*, crayfish
    powder
1 to 2 peppers (optional)
1 small Maggi cube
½ cup palm oil, palm kernel oil, or sesame oil

Pemahuin

1. Rinse potato leaves and put into a colander. Leave aside so that water continues to drain off.
2. Add water and garden eggs to a large pot and cook over high heat for 10 minutes or until tender. Remove garden eggs and set aside in a bowl. Leave the pot over high heat.
3. Wash rice, drain off water and add to the pot. Stir thoroughly but gently using wooden spoon to prevent rice from breaking or sticking together. Cover with a tight-fitting lid and cook for 10 minutes or until most of the water evaporates.
4. Put potato leaves over the rice. Place whole pepper, garden eggs, ground ogiri (or a substitute), and Maggi over the potato leaves. Cover quickly with the tight-fitting lid and cook over high heat for 5 minutes to generate enough steam.
5. Reduce heat to low and simmer for 15 to 20 minutes or until the potato leaves are soft and properly steamed. Remove garden eggs, pepper, and ogiri (or a substitute) but leave rice covered over the low heat. Mash garden eggs, pepper and ogiri separately into a fine blend and add to the potato leaves and put all these ingredients into a small pot.
6. Add oil (palm oil, palm kernel oil, sesame oil, or your favorite cooking oil) and bring the small pot to a boil over medium heat. Taste and add more salt if desired.
7. Reduce heat to low and simmer for 5 minutes or until the sauce starts to stick to the bottom of the pot. Then remove rice from pot and spread out onto an open dish. The rice should be fluffy, separated from each other, tender and dry.

Serve rice and sauce hot. If you are not in the vegetarian mood, serve with whole fried fish or fried herring.

Variations: Italian Spinach: Pemahuin cooked with Italian Spinach.

Prepare this dish using the *Pemahuin* recipe, but replace the potato leaves with Italian spinach.

PILLAAH VEGGIE SAUCE

SERVES 6 to 7

INGREDIENTS

3 bundles *pillaah*
3 cups water
2 medium eggplants or 6 green garden eggs
1 cup boiled beans (optional)
1 cup okra, finely chopped into 2-inch rings
½ cup mushroom, finely diced
1 cup palm oil
1 to 4 peppers, ground or whole (optional)
1 medium onion, ground or whole (optional)
1 small Maggi
½ teaspoon salt or to taste

1. Wash *pillaah* and separate the green leaves from the large spine in the middle. Chop into large chunks. Chop leaves and spine separately. Add water to each and rinse. Drain off water and keep leaves and spine in separate bowls.
2. Put water into a large pot. Add large spine, eggplants (or garden eggs), and beans. Cook over high heat for 5 minutes.
3. Add the *pillaah* leaves, okra, and mushroom. Bring to a boil.
4. Add palm oil and cook for 20 minutes. Add pepper, onion, Maggi, and salt. Bring to a boil.
5. Taste and add more salt if desired. Reduce heat and simmer for 5 to 10 minutes or until sauce is thick.

Serve hot with steamed rice.

Variation: Collard Green: Prepare this sauce using the *Pillaah Sauce* recipe, but replace the *pillaah* leaf with collard green.

BLACK-EYED BEANS VEGGIE SAUCE

SERVES 6 to 8

INGREDIENTS

2 cups black-eyed beans, washed and cooked until tender
1 cup palm oil
1 medium onions, finely chopped
1 small Maggi cube
½ teaspoon salt
1 to 2 hot peppers, ground or whole (optional)

1. Make sure beans are extremely soft, almost pulp like, and set aside in its stock. (Use pressure cooker, if possible.)
2. Pour palm oil into a large pot and heat over medium. Add onion and fry until soft. Add beans along with its stock and bring to a boil.
3. Add Maggi, salt, and pepper. Cover and bring to a boil. Cook for 10 minutes. Taste and add more salt if desired.
4. Reduce heat to low and simmer until sauce is thick and about to stick to the bottom of the pot.

Serve with boiled or fried plantain or with any of your favorite boiled tubers.

Variation: Black-eyed Beans with Other Oils: Prepare this sauce using the *Black-eyed Beans* recipe, but replace the palm oil with your favorite cooking oil.

Veggie black eyed beans with boiled cassava

OKRA VEGGIE SAUCE

SERVES 6 to 8

INGREDIENTS

4 cups water
2 medium eggplants or 6 garden eggs, peeled, chopped into small cubes, seeds removed
3 cups fresh tender okra, finely chopped
¾ teaspoon salt or to taste
1 cup palm oil
1 cup beans
1 medium onion, finely chopped
4 hot peppers, ground or whole (optional)
1 cup diced mushroom
1 small Maggi to taste

1. Add water to a pot. Add garden eggs (or eggplant) and bring to a boil over high heat. Add okra and sprinkle salt over it. Cover and continue to cook for 10 minutes, then add palm oil and beans and bring to a boil.
2. Add onion, pepper, mushroom and Maggi. Cover and cook for 10 minutes. Avoid stirring as much as possible; instead, shake pot occasionally to prevent okra from sticking to the bottom of the pot or breaking up into pulp. Taste and add more salt if desired.
3. Reduce heat to low and simmer for 20 minutes or until sauce is thick and about to stick to the bottom of the pot.

Serve hot with steamed rice, *fufu*, or pounded yam.

GARDEN EGGS DELIGHT

SERVES 4

INGREDIENTS

2 cups garden eggs
2 cups water
1 to 2 peppers, whole (optional)
1 teaspoon salt or to taste
1 small Maggi cube
¼ cup palm oil

1. Remove the stalk from the garden eggs, wash, and put into a pot. Add pepper and water and bring to a boil over medium heat. Continue to Cook until garden eggs and pepper are soft and water evaporates.
2. Put garden eggs and pepper into a bowl, add salt and mash all the ingredients together. Continue to mash together or blend until everything becomes an evenly mixed pulp.
3. Return the mashed ingredients to the pot. Add Maggi and oil, cover and cook over medium heat for 5 minutes.
4. Taste and add more salt if desired. Reduce heat to low and simmer for 5 more minutes.

Serve hot with okra rice or your favorite boiled tuber.

Variation: Garden Eggs with Other Oils

Prepare this dish using the *Garden Eggs Delight* Recipe, but replace the palm oil with your favorite vegetable oil.

Main Dishes: Rice and Other Grains

Rice is a staple food in many countries in the region. Millet, sorghum, and couscous are other types of grains that are eaten in the region, although not as extensively as rice. Millet is also a staple in parts of Northern Nigeria, Niger, Mali and Burkina Faso. Couscous, a grain-based food made from grains such as millet, wheat and sorghum is a very healthy dish and is quite popular in the region.

"Country Rice" (Uncooked)

Various rice dishes. From left steamed rice, right, check rice, top Joloff rice

Main Dishes: Rice and Other Grains

Rice

Boiled or Steamed Rice
Variation: New rice
Boiled Rice with Okra
Crain-Crain or *Check* Rice
Variation: Spinach and Okra
Variation: Hibiscus Leaves
Variation: Frozen *Jute* Leaves
Joloff Rice
Coconut Rice

Other Grains

Couscous
Variation: Joloff Couscous
Boiled Millet

Food Story

Abundant Food in the Midst of None

NOTE ABOUT PARBOILED RICE: Cook parboiled rice for all the recipes in this book following the recipe for the type of rice you will be cooking but add 2½ cups water to every 1 cup of rice.

HOW TO COOK RICE: There are many types of rice, and sometimes the well-accepted measurement of 1 cup of rice to 1¼ cups of water may not work with some grains. For this reason, it is a good idea to know the old, traditional, helpful tips about cooking rice:

While cooking rice or other grains, always use a wooden spoon to mix. This will prevent the rice from breaking and/or sticking at the bottom of the pot. Keep the pot covered while the rice cooks to retain the steam and cut down on the cooking time.

To confirm that rice has cooked to the point where you can reduce the heat, pick a grain and press it between two fingers. The rice should be soft, with a little hard part in the middle. At this stage, let the rice simmer. The rice will be well cooked and fluffy, without any hard part in the middle. If this occurs, you know that you have properly cooked it.

Before removing cooked rice from the fire, check to confirm that it is dry. Test its dryness by putting a wooden spoon through the rice, from the top to the bottom. If the spoon is dry, this means the rice is cooked, dry, and ready to serve. If the spoon is wet, keep the rice over low heat until it is done.

Alternatively, rice can be cooked in a rice cooker. To prepare, follow instructions on the rice cooker and the rice packet.

Where recipes in this book ask for testing to see if rice is cooked, the information here should be the guide.

BOILED OR STEAMED RICE

SERVES 4

INGREDIENTS

½ teaspoon salt or to taste (optional)
2½ cups water
2 cups rice, regular rice, not parboiled

1. In a large pot, add salt and water. Bring to a boil over high heat.
2. Wash rice once, drain, and add to the pot. Stir thoroughly using wooden spoon to prevent rice from sticking together or to the bottom of the pot.
3. Cover with a tight-fitting lid. Continue to cook for 10 to 15 minutes or until water can no longer be seen on top of rice.
4. Stir slowly and gently with the wooden spoon. Cover, reduce heat to low, and cook for 15 to 20 minutes or until rice is cooked and ready. It should be tender, fluffy and dry.

Serve hot with soup, stew, or mixed sauce.

Variation: New Rice: During the harvest months in Sierra Leone, the newly harvested long-grain rice can be processed to give off a nice and unique aroma. To create this, simply wash rice once, drain off the water, put the rice in a pot and put over medium heat. With a wooden spoon, start stirring immediately and continue until rice is dry, shiny and light brown with special nutty aroma. Remove from heat. Using the same measurement of 2 cups rice to 2½ cups water, add the rice and water to pot and continue to cook following the procedure for *Boiled or Steamed Rice.*

BOILED RICE WITH OKRA: This type of rice includes a small amount of okra, which makes the rice slippery and delicious.

SERVES 4

INGREDIENTS

2½ cups water
6 pods of okra, grated or ground, set aside in a covered bowl
2 cups rice, long-grain
½ teaspoon salt

1. Add water to a pot and bring to a boil over high heat. Pour small amount of boiling water over ground okra. Keep the pot, with the remaining boiling water, over high heat.
2. Wash rice once, drain, and add to the pot. With wooden spoon, stir thoroughly and gently to prevent rice from sticking together or to the bottom of the pot. Cover with a tight-fitting lid and cook over high heat for 10 minutes or until a very small amount of water can be seen at the top of the rice.
3. Mix together the okra and the water in the bowl until water and okra blends evenly. Pour the mixed okra over the top of the rice. Cover quickly to keep the steam in the pot. Reduce heat to medium and continue to cook for 5 minutes.
4. Reduce heat to low and continue to cook for 20 to 30 minutes or until rice is cooked. It should be fluffy, dry and tender. Remove okra from the top of the rice and put into a large bowl. Add salt and stir vigorously with wooden spoon to ensure it is a smooth pulp.
5. Remove rice from the pot and add to okra. Stir okra with the rice until both are evenly mixed.

Serve hot with soup or stew.

Alternatively, add water and okra to a pot and cook over high heat for 10 minutes. Remove okra, add salt, and blend or beat vigorously to a pulp. Cook rice until it is fluffy. Remove from pot and mix thoroughly with the okra. Serve hot.

Another way of cooking this rice dish is to boil the okra separately and then blend or mix to a pulp. Cook the rice in a rice cooker. Then, mix in the okra and serve.

***CRAIN-CRAIN* OR *CHECK* RICE*:** The people in the east and south of Sierra Leone are known to have perfected this dish. I am not an exception. When cooked, this rice gives an appearance that looks like a green-and-white-checkered material. It is a great dish that is well loved, particularly in Sierra Leone. The *crain-crain* added is minimal. (In the absence of *crain-crain*, fresh or frozen *jute* leaves or a combination of okra and spinach can be used to achieve the same result.)

It is important to cook this dish using a large pot. This will prevent the *crain-crain* from spilling over while it is cooking over the rice.

CRAIN-CRAIN OR *CHECK* RICE

INGREDIENTS

SERVES 6 to 8

1 bundle or 1 handful of *crain-crain*, finely chopped, to measure 1 cup
A pinch of bicarbonate of soda
2½ cups water
2 cups rice, long-grain
½ teaspoon salt or to taste

1. Add *crain-crain* to a bowl and then add bicarbonate of soda. Cover and keep aside. Add water to a large pot and bring to a boil over high heat. Pour small amount of boiled water over the *crain-crain* (enough to cover it by 1 inch).
2. Using a wooden spoon, stir *crain-crain* vigorously with the hot water and the bicarbonate of soda until all blends in evenly. Keep the mixture covered in the bowl.
3. Wash rice once, drain, and then add to the remaining boiling water in the pot. With wooden spoon, stir thoroughly but gently to prevent rice from sticking together or to the bottom of the pot. Cover with a tight-fitting lid and bring to a boil. Continue to cook for 10 to 15 minutes or until very little water can be seen at the top of the rice.
4. Pour the *crain-crain* mixture over the rice and cover quickly with tight-fitting lid. Reduce heat to medium and continue to cook for 5 minutes.
5. Reduce heat to low and cook for 20 to 30 minutes or until *crain-crain* is properly steamed and rice is dry, tender and fluffy. Remove *crain-crain* from the top of the rice and place into a large bowl. Add salt and stir vigorously with wooden spoon, then add to rice and continue to stir to ensure both rice and crain-crain blend evenly.

Serve hot with soup or stew.

There are other ways of cooking *check rice*. You can use spinach and okra or jute leaves and okra if the fresh crain-crain leaves are not available. Sometimes but quite seldom, people have used the young leaves of the hibiscus plant to prepare check rice. For all of these variations, first cook the rice using the rice cooker or the traditional method until the rice is fluffy. Then prepare spinach or the alternative vegetables that are available and mix with the fluffy rice.

Variation: Spinach and Okra: In the absence of *crain-crain,* you can use spinach and okra, (fresh or frozen) to cook this dish. If using frozen spinach, do not wash the leaves, just defrost and steam and if using frozen okra, add to the pot in its frozen state and cook. To cook this dish, start by cooking the rice separately using the rice cooker or the procedure for *Boiled or Steamed Rice.* Next, wash the spinach and put it into a pot and steam. Then clean the fresh okra cut off the end and the top and cook in enough water to cover it by 2 inches. Cook okra for 10 minutes or until okra is soft and water evaporates. Then remove the boiled okra from the pot and add it to the steamed spinach. Blend them together to create a fine purée. Put the mixture in a large bowl and stir in cooked fluffy rice.

Variation: Hibiscus Leaves: Cook this following the cooking procedure above for spinach and okra but replace the spinach with a bundle of young hibiscus leaves.

Variation: Frozen jute leaves: As pointed out earlier, jute leaf is another name for crain-crain. In its frozen state, I have found out that sometimes it is not as slippery as the fresh crain-crain. Therefore, whenever I use it to cook check rice, I combine the jute leaves with some okra. Cook this dish following the recipe for spinach and okra variety but replace the spinach with a packet of frozen jute leaves.

JOLOFF RICE: *Joloff* rice is usually served with stews and vegetables. It is a favored dish in many of the countries in West Africa. Cooking methods may vary slightly, but it is common knowledge that the secret to good, tasty *joloff* rice lies in the stock used to prepare the rice. It is good practice to prepare your stock before you begin cooking the rice or prepare it well in advance and keep it refrigerated to use when needed. (See the *Planning and Preparing Ahead* chapter for the stock recipe.) In the absence of homemade stock, Campbell's broth is also quite good.

This dish is believed to have originated among the Wolof people of Senegal and Gambia, and the original name was *djolof* rice. Today, it is such a popular dish in the entire region that many of the countries believe it originated from their end of the region.

JOLOFF RICE

SERVES 6

INGREDIENTS

4 tablespoons vegetable cooking oil
1 large onion, finely chopped
2 cloves garlic, finely chopped
1 large tomato, finely chopped
2½ cups stock, chicken beef or vegetable)
2 teaspoons tomato paste
1 small Maggi cube
½ teaspoon salt or to taste
2 cups rice, long-grain rice
1 large pepper (optional)
2 bay leaves

Joloff rice served with beef stewed and steamed cabbage

1. In a skillet, heat the vegetable oil over medium heat. Toss in onion and garlic and stir continuously until both are soft. Then add tomato and continue to fry until tomato appears soft. Remove from heat. Add stock to a large pot and transfer content from skillet to the pot. Add tomato paste, Maggi, and salt. Cover and bring to a boil over high heat.
2. Wash rice once, drain, and then add to the pot. Stir very well with wooden spoon to prevent rice from sticking together or to the bottom of the pot. Cover with a tight-fitting lid and bring to a boil. Cook for 5 minutes and then reduce heat to medium.
3. Stir slowly and gently with wooden spoon. Taste and add more salt, if necessary. Place bay leaves and whole pepper on top of the rice. Cover and cook for 5 to 10 minutes or until water evaporates. Reduce heat to low and continue to cook for 10 minutes or until rice is completely cooked, dry, and fluffy. Remove pot from heat.
4. Remove bay leaves from top and discard. Using wooden spoon, remove rice from pot and spread rice out onto an open dish.

Serve with any of the regular stews included in this cookbook. (See recipes for regular stews in the *Main Dishes: Stews and Spicy Fish* chapter.) Serve this with a generous heaping of your favorite steamed vegetable. Also add few slices of fried plantain, if you prefer.

COCONUT RICE

SERVES 4

INGREDIENTS

1 dry coconut, grated
2 plus 2 cups water, boiled
1 ginger, grated
½ teaspoon salt
1 tablespoon tomato paste
2 tablespoons cooking oil
1 medium onion, finely chopped
2 cloves garlic, ground or crushed
2 cups rice, long-grain
1 hot pepper (optional)

1. Add grated coconut to 2 cups boiling water and stir. Cover and keep for 5 minutes. Put a sieve over a large bowl and sieve the coconut to extract the liquid. Wash repeatedly with the remaining 2 cups of water until most of the coconut milk is extracted from the shaft. Discard shaft and pour coconut liquid into a pot. Then add ginger, salt, and tomato paste. Bring to a boil.
2. Then, in a skillet, heat oil over medium heat. Add onion and garlic and fry until the onions are soft and shiny. Add to coconut liquid in the pot. Bring to a boil and continue to cook over high heat until the liquid goes down by half (measuring 2 cups).
3. Wash rice once, drain, and add to the pot. With a wooden spoon, stir thoroughly but gently to prevent rice from breaking or from sticking together at the bottom of pot. Taste and add more salt if desired. Cover with a tight-fitting lid and bring to a boil. Cook for 5 minutes and then reduce heat to medium. Continue to cook for 5 to 10 minutes or until water evaporates.
4. Reduce heat to low and continue to cook for 10 minutes or until rice is completely cooked, dry, and fluffy. Remove rice from pot and spread out onto an open dish.

Serve with any of the regular stews included in this cookbook. (See recipes for regular stews in the *Main Dishes: Stews and Spicy Fish* chapter.) Serve this with a generous heaping of your favorite steamed vegetable. Also add few slices of fried plantain, if you prefer.

Couscous is a popular dish in the region. Its production process can however be time consuming and labor-intensive. Thankfully, couscous can now be mass produced using machines thus encouraging its commercialization and distribution. The finished product is always pre-steamed and dried and packed for sale with cooking instructions on the package. This has made it possible to have couscous throughout the world and the detailed cooking instructions on the packages have made couscous cooking easy. The recipe in this book is simply the way I cook the commercially produced couscous.

COUSCOUS

SERVES 4

INGREDIENTS

3 cups water or stock
¼ teaspoon salt
2 cups couscous

Add salt and water or stock to pot and bring to a boil over high heat. Stir in the couscous. Reduce heat to low and simmer for 5 to 10 minutes or until couscous is dry, soft and fluffy.

Serve with spicy chicken stew.

Variation: Joloff Couscous: Prepare this dish using the *Joloff Rice recipe*, except use 1½ cups stock per 1 cup couscous.

Serve with any of the regular stews included in this cookbook. (See recipes for regular stews in the *Main Dishes: Stews and Spicy Fish* chapter.) Serve this with a generous heaping of your favorite steamed vegetable.

BOILED MILLET: These very little yellow grains, which have a tiny dot on one side, are very nutritious. Millet is eaten in the region and in some countries in the region such as Mali, some parts of Northern Nigeria, Niger and Burkina Faso, it is a staple.

BOILED MILLET

SERVES 4

INGREDIENTS

2 cups millet
2½ cups water or stock
¼ teaspoon salt

1. Add millet to a skillet, put over medium heat, and stir continuously for 5 minutes or until millet appears shiny and golden in color and gives off a nice, nutty aroma.
2. Add water or stock to pot and bring to a boil over high heat. Add millet, bring to a boil, reduce heat and simmer for 20 minutes or until it is dry, soft, and fluffy.

Serve with spicy chicken stew or any of the regular stews; see recipes for regular stews in the *Main Dishes: Stews and Spicy Fish* chapter), steamed vegetables, or mixed sauces.

Food Story: Abundant Food in the Midst of None

Cassava is a plant for all seasons. The plant itself is a woody shrub that is easy to grow. Once planted, it requires very little attention. The cassava plant is drought resistant and easy to nurture; it grows year-round and is available in all seasons, whether dry, rainy, hot, or cold. The leaves contain a large supply of rich proteins, vitamins, and minerals and it serves as an important vegetable in the West African Region. The cassava tubers are a major source of carbohydrate. The mature cassava tuber can be preserved underground for several months. In a region where food shortages occur often, we, in Sierra Leone and some other countries in West Africa are still blessed to have a plant that, if cultivated with some seriousness, can provide a healthy and balanced diet – proteins, vitamins, and minerals from its leaves and ample carbohydrates from its tubers.

However, most of the women in the southern part of Sierra Leone understand the importance of the cassava tuber and its leaves, and they use it well. Likewise, in many parts of the region, people do not consider themselves fed until they have eaten rice. However, rice growing is difficult and time-consuming, and rice is prone to shortages. Perhaps we, in Sierra Leone and many other countries in the region, would be in a better position, nationally and regionally, if we emulated these wise women of the southern region and adopt the entire cassava as a major and essential food item.

I recall, with fond memories, my childhood days in some of the towns and villages in southern Sierra Leone. To this day, I am still fascinated by the commendable methods of the women, in the villages around Lake Mabesi and Lake Mapie in southern Sierra Leone, who used cassava to ensure people were fed properly. The following is an account of what I saw when the women of Njala (located near Lake Mabesi, in southern Sierra Leone) used cassava to keep hunger at bay.

Each day, the women brought out their share of cassava tubers that had been harvested the previous day and piled them together at the 'cooking point.' This was a large, airy backyard space that was dominated by coffee trees and filled with noisy scavenger monkeys. These animals would steal pieces of cassava from the ground and climb into the trees to sit comfortably and eat their prize. Various birds flew in and out from the trees and the monkeys' noise seemed to blend harmoniously with the birdsongs.

At the cooking point, the women gathered around the cassava tubers with knives in both hands. They joyfully talked and gossiped as they peeled the cassava tubers and then dumped the peeled cassava tubers into a large container full of water. Afterward, they took the peeled skin to Lake Mabesi, which was located just below the cooking point, and placed the cassava skin around the edge of the lake.

Once this was completed, they returned to the cooking point where they chopped the cassava into smaller pieces. The cassava was rinsed and then added to a giant pot along with enough clean cold water to cover the cassava. They then placed the pot over three large stones in triangular formation. Underneath the stones, a huge fire would be roaring.

While the cassava was cooking, the women took their fishing nets back to the lake to the place where they had earlier deposited the cassava skins. They quietly entered the lake and circled the nets around the cassava skins. They held onto the nets and then moved the nets slowly and quietly to completely surround the cassava skins. When the tiny, tasty fish, which were feeding on the cassava skins, attempted to swim away when they felt the women's presence, it was too late. All the fish easily landed in the nets. The women collected their catch of the day and returned to the cooking point to prepare one large pot of fish soup.

When the cassava was cooked, the women washed, rinsed, and poured plenty of cold water over it. The cassava was then served with the fish. There was always plenty of boiled cassava and fish soup left in the pot. This was covered and left, for the whole day, so that anyone, including passersby, could feed on the cassava and fish soup.

Fish eggs were also plentiful, and sometimes these were seasoned with salt and steamed and smoked over an open fire. These were left, covered, on a locally-made, open oven near the cassava. They were eaten with the cassava whenever someone in the community was hungry.

Main Dishes: Tubers and Tree Crops Dishes

These are prepared using the boiling, frying, or roasting methods. The roasted ones are very often eaten as snacks (see the *Snacks and Accompaniments* chapter for recipes). The boiled and fried ones are eaten either alone as a snack or as a main meal with any steamed vegetables and any of the following: fried fish, beef, chicken, shrimp, stews, and soups.

Cooking time for all boiled tubers and tree crops vary, depending on the type, age, and size.

Boiled tuber and Tree crop	Large Chunks of Boiled Cassava
	Variation: Small Slices
	Boiled Sweet Potatoes, Yam, Cocoyam, Plantain, Breadfruit (peeled)
	Boiled Sweet Potatoes (unpeeled)
	Other Boiled Tubers and Tree Crops (unpeeled)
	Partee
Fried tuber and Tree crop	Fried Cassava
	Fried Yam
	Fried Plantains, Potatoes
Gari* and *Attieke	*Gari* Dish
	Variation: Soft and Fluffy *Gari*
	Attieke Dish
Fufu	*Domba*
	Fufu
	Tuei
	Yam *Fufu*
	Fufu Combo

LARGE CHUNKS OF BOILED CASSAVA

SERVES 4

INGREDIENTS

2 medium cassava tubers
Water, enough to cover cassava tubers, about 3 inches or more
Salt, to taste

1. Peel the cassava tubers, cut into medium sizes, and wash thoroughly in cold water.
2. Put into pot with water to cover. Add salt, cover with a tight-fitting lid, and boil for 30 minutes or until soft. (Cooking time varies according to type, age, and size.)
3. Test with a toothpick or fork, cassava is cooked if it is soft and tender.

Serve with soup, fried whole fish, or fried chicken and steamed vegetables on the side. Alternatively, if you add salt and butter or palm oil, the boiled cassava can also serve as a snack.

Variation: Small Slices: Prepare this dish using the *Large Chunk Boiled Cassava* recipe, but make sure to cut the cassava tubers into small slices.

BOILED SWEET POTATOES, YAM, COCOYAM, PLANTAIN, BREADFRUIT (PEELED): Prepare these using the *Large Chunk Boiled Cassava* recipe, but replace the cassava with the tuber of your choice. Unlike cassava, these can be boiled in their skins (see the example in the *Boiled Sweet Potatoes* recipe, below.)

BOILED SWEET POTATOES (UNPEELED)

SERVES 2

INGREDIENTS

4 medium potatoes
Water, enough to cover potatoes by 3 inches or more

1. Wash potatoes until they are very clean. Cut potatoes into halves or leave whole and then place into a large pot.
2. Add water and boil for 30 minutes or until soft. Remove from pot.
3. Allow to cool. Remove skin and cut into slices.

Serve with black-eyed beans sauce, groundnut soup, stew, or pepper soup.

OTHER BOILED TUBERS AND TREE CROPS (UNPEELED): Like sweet potatoes, plantains, unripe bananas, breadfruit, and yam, there are other tubers and tree crops that can be boiled in their skin. Boil these unpeeled as in the *Boiled Sweet Potatoes* recipe, Peel before serving.

PARTEE: This can be prepared with three or more tubers and combined with other ingredients like plantains, mangoes, and smoked dry fish. The number of tubers used is a matter of preference, but it will come out nicer if ripe plantains or mangoes are also added. Likewise, palm oil or groundnut paste can be added, but not both.

If served as a snack, eat only a very small portion. This meal can be heavy and too much can fill you up, much like a main meal would.

SERVES 6 to 8

INGREDIENTS

3 cups water
1 medium cassava tuber, peeled and chopped into medium chunks
1 medium yam, peeled and chopped into large chunks
2 small cocoyam, peeled and chopped into medium chunks
2 sweet potatoes, peeled and chopped into large chunks
1 ripe plantain, peeled and chopped into large chunks
1 cup large smoked fish flakes, from snapper, tilapia, catfish, or barracuda (optional)
1 small onion, finely chopped
1 to 2 peppers, ground or whole (optional)
Salt to taste
1 small Maggi
½ cup palm oil or 3 tablespoons groundnut paste
1 ripe mango, peeled and sliced, into medium pieces

1. Add water and cassava to a large pot. Bring to a boil. Add yam, cocoyam, potatoes, plantain, and cook for 5 minutes.
2. Add fish flakes, onion, pepper, salt, Maggi and palm oil (if using groundnut paste instead of palm oil, mix the groundnut paste with some water to form a smooth liquid and add).
3. Add slices of mango and bring to a boil. Taste and add more salt if desired.
4. Reduce heat to low and cook for 20 minutes or until liquid around the ingredients is slightly thick.

Serve hot with a bowl of garden salad.

Partee dish

FRIED CASSAVA

SERVES 4

INGREDIENTS

2 medium cassava tubers
2 cups water, to boil cassava tubers
Salt to taste
½ cup cooking oil
1 medium onion, finely chopped
2 cloves garlic, finely chopped
4 tablespoons water
1 large pepper (optional

1. Peel the cassava tubers, cut into large chunks, wash and drain off the water. Put cassava into pot, add water and salt. Cover with a tight-fitting lid and boil for 30 minutes or until soft.
2. Remove pot from heat, put cassava into colander to drain off water. Rinse with cold water. Leave cassava in colander so that water continues to drain off.
3. In a large skillet, heat oil over medium heat. Add onion and garlic and sauté for 5 minutes or until soft. Place boiled cassava slices neatly in layers over the onion and garlic and then sprinkle with salt and bring to a boil. Reduce heat to low and with a wooden spoon gently move the other ingredients so that they are on top of the cassava. Continue to cook until all ingredients are slightly brown.
4. Add water and put whole pepper on top. Cover and bring to a boil. Taste and add more salt if desired.
5. Reduce heat to low and cook for 10 minutes or until most of the liquid around the ingredients evaporates.

Serve with whole fried fish and steamed vegetable of your choice.

FRIED YAM: Prepare this dish using the *Fried Cassava* recipe, but replace the cassava tuber with yam.

FRIED PLANTAINS, POTATOES: These can be eaten either as a main dish or as a snack. The recipes for these are therefore in the *Snacks and Accompaniments* chapter

To eat as a main meal, serve with black eyed beans sauce.

GARI AND ATTIEKE: *Gari,* also known as *Farina* and *Attieke* are produced from grated cassava tubers. *Gari* and *Attieke* both have a couscous-like grain appearance but *Attieke* is more refined than *Gari.* Both foods are popular dishes in the region. In Côte d'Ivoire, *Attieke* is a staple. These cassava products are available in the region and in Asian and other ethnic food stores in many countries outside the region. Cooking these food items does not take a long time and sometimes some of those sold in food stores comes with cooking instructions.

GARI DISH

SERVES 4

INGREDIENTS

2 cups water
Salt to taste
1½ cups *gari*

1. Pour water into a pot and bring to a boil over high heat.
2. Reduce heat to low. Add salt. Sprinkle *gari* over boiling water.
3. Stir vigorously using a wooden spoon until dough is soft and smooth.
4. Mold into 4 balls.

Serve with stew.

Variation: Soft and Fluffy Gari: This dish is cooked with less water, 1 cup *Gari* to 1 cup water. Boil the water, pour into a large mixing bowl, and sprinkle 2 cups of *gari* over it. Stir well with a wooden spoon until it is evenly mixed. Cover the bowl and let stand for 20 minutes. *Gari* will be fluffy and soft. Fluffy *Gari* is a popular quick meal in the region particularly among children in boarding schools. In the schools, the children usually add a cup of cold water to two cups Gari and after mixing they let it stand for longer than 20 minutes in order to get it to be soft and fluffy. They usually add a tin of sardine and some pepper to the sardine and then eat or they can add sugar and eat. I tried this so many times as a child when I was at a boarding school

Serve with stew. Alternatively add sugar or sardine and serve.

ATTIEKE DISH

SERVES 4

INGREDIENTS

2 cups a*ttieke*
2 cups water

1. Pour water into a pot and bring to a boil over high heat. Remove pot from heat. Add *attieke* to the water in the pot and stir gently. Cover and leave to stand for 10 minutes.
2. Place pot over low heat and cook for 5 to 10 minutes or until *attieke* is warm and fluffy. As it cooks, stir continuously with a fork to separate the grains.

Serve with fried fish and steamed vegetables or green salad. Alternatively, serve with spicy chicken stew or any of the regular stews (see recipes for regular stews in the *Main Dishes: Stews and Spicy Fish* chapter), together with steamed vegetables, or mixed sauces. It can also be served as a side dish for a salad.

FUFU: *Fufu* is a major staple in the region and is made from selected tubers and tree crops. In the tuber category is cassava, yam and cocoyam and in the tree crop category is plantain and corn. Fufu can be made with either a tuber, tree crop, or a combination of multiple tubers and/or tree crops. To cook fufu, the tuber or tree crop has to be first prepared either through grating and fermenting, or through boiling and pounding. For example, cassava fufu can be made with fermented cassava tuber or by boiling and pounding the tuber using a mortar and pestle. Other kinds of fufu can also be made by boiling tubers and tree crops and pounding them either separately or together using a mortar and pestle.

In Sierra Leone and Liberia, cassava tuber is made into a type of fufu called *domba* using the boiling and pounding method. In both countries, fufu is also made from grated and fermented cassava. In Ghana and neighboring countries, a combination of cassava and plantain, or yam and plantain, is usually boiled and pounded into fufu. In Ghana, a special type of fufu called *Banku* is also made from fermented corn.

Fufu made using the traditional means of first boiling and pounding the tuber or tree crop or grating and fermenting can be time consuming and the end product can have a very short shelf life. Thankfully, fufu production has now been commercialized. It is produced in powdered/flour form and is available in the region and in Asian and other ethnic food stores in many countries outside the region. In the food stores, they can be labeled as flour, powdered or pounded. For example you can find yam flour labeled as yam powder, yam flour or pounded yam. They are only different in names but they are all the same things.

In Sierra Leone and Liberia, long before the commercialized production of cassava in a powdered/flour form started, people were making cassava into the powdered/flour form which they called *tuei.* The production involved peeling the cassava, chopping it into medium pieces, washing and drying in the sun, and pounding using a mortar and pestle. This is perhaps why most people in the rural areas of Sierra Leone still refer to the commercially produced powdered cassava as *tuei.* The main difference between *tuei* and non-fermented fufu is that instead of boiling the cassava after peeling and chopping, you dry the cassava instead.

DOMBA *(fufu from boiled tuber)*

SERVES 6

INGREDIENTS

4 medium cassava tubers
Water, for boiling cassava
Mortar
Pestle

1. Peel the cassava tubers, cut into large chunks, wash and drain off the water. Put cassava into pot, add water and salt. Cover with a tight-fitting lid and boil for 30 minutes or until soft.
2. Remove pot from heat, put cassava into colander to drain off water. Rinse with cold water.
3. Add to mortar and pound with a pestle until it is soft, thick, and smooth. If it sticks to the pestle, add a few drops of water and continue to pound until the consistency is soft and smooth, with no lumps.
4. Remove from mortar, divide into six small portions, and mold into separate balls.

Serve with any slippery sauce, soups, bitter leaf, sorrel leaf, sorrel flower, or cocoyam leaf.

FUFU *(fufu from cassava tuber)*

SERVES 6

INGREDIENTS

3 cups water
4 cups fufu

1. In a pot, add 2 cups water to *fufu* and mix well. Sieve over a pot and then discard the hard parts that are left in the sieve.
2. In a large pot, bring sieved mixture to a boil over medium heat and stir continuously with wooden spoon.
3. If *fufu* is too hard, add a little bit of water from time to time.
4. Continue to cook until color changes and *fufu* becomes waterless, smooth dough.
5. Remove from heat. Divide into 6 pieces and roll into balls.

Serve with bitter leaf, sorrel leaf, *egusi* soup, groundnut soup, or any of the slippery sauces.

TUEI *(traditionally made cassava flour fufu)*

SERVES 4

INGREDIENTS

2 cups cassava flour
3 cups water

1. In a pot, mix cassava flour with water and place over medium heat. Mix continuously and vigorously with a wooden spoon until it starts to become stiff.
2. Reduce heat to low. Continue to mix until all the water evaporates and the mold is smooth and soft. If it is not smooth and soft, add more water and continue to mix until you get it right. (The dough like cassava will give off a smell quite different from the smell of the raw powder.)
3. Remove from the pot and divide into sections. Mold into 4 balls.

Serve with bitter leaf, sorrel leaf, *egusi* soup, groundnut soup, or any of the slippery sauces.

COMMERCIALLY PRODUCED POWDERED/FLOUR FOR FUFU: As already pointed out, cassava, yam, cocoyam, plantain and corn are available in powdered/flour form. Each of these can be used to cook *fufu* or you can combine any two to make your favorite *fufu*. Cooking procedures for these powdered/flour *fufu* products are all the same. The two recipes in this book for yam Flour *fufu* and the combination of cassava and plantain flour *fufu* are only examples of how these commercially produced products are cooked.

YAM FUFU *(fufu from yam flour)*

SERVES 4

INGREDIENTS

3 cups water
2 cups yam flour

1. In a pot, bring water to a boil over medium heat.
2. Sprinkle on the yam flour and stir continuously with a wooden spoon until it becomes thick.
3. Reduce heat to low. Cover and cook for 5 minutes. Stir again until the mold is soft and smooth.
4. Mold into 4 balls.

Serve with bitter leaf, sorrel leaf, *egusi* soup, groundnut soup, or any of the slippery sauces.

FUFU **COMBO** (fufu from combination of two or more flour such as cassava and plantain flour combined)

SERVES 4

INGREDIENTS

1 cups cassava flour
1 cup plantain flour
3 cups water
1 cups cassava flour
1 cup plantain flour

1. Combine cassava and plantain flour in a bowl and mix using a spoon so that both blend evenly.
2. In a pot, bring water to a boil over medium heat.
3. Sprinkle on the combined flour and stir continuously with a wooden spoon until it becomes thick.
4. Reduce heat to low. Cover and cook for 5 minutes. Mix again until the mold is soft and smooth.
5. Mold into 4 balls.

Snacks and Accompaniments

Snack tray. From bottom, fried plantains, center line displayed on green spinach leaves is Oleleh cooked with corn beef, left fish balls, right beans Akara.

SNACKS: These can be eaten anytime of the day. For people who like appetizers before a meal, rice *akara*, fried herring bites, beans *akara,* fried green plantain, fish balls, crab meat balls, roasted groundnut, and boiled groundnut can be served for this purpose.

Snacks and Accompaniments

Accompaniment Hot Pepper Sauce
Variations: Vegetarian

Snack Rice Pap
Rice *Kanya*
Variation: *Farina/Gari*
Rice *Akara*
Variation: Other Types of Flour
Boiled Groundnut
Roasted Groundnut
Groundnut Cake
Benniseed Cake
Coconut Cake
Fish Balls
Crab Balls
Fried Herring Bites
Variation: In Batter
Roast Beef on Skewers
Beans *Akara* and *Oleleh*
Beans *Akara*
Oleleh/Moin-Moin
Variation: Other Oils
Fried Snacks
Fried Ripe Plantain
Fried Green Plantain
Fried Green Banana
Fried Sweet Potato
Fried Breadfruit
Roasted/Grilled Tubers and Tree Crops
Roasted Breadfruit
Roasted Sweet Potato
Roasted Plantain
Roasted Cassava Tuber

Food Story The Lessons in Tolerance

HOT PEPPER SAUCE: Hot pepper sauce is a good accompaniment that goes very well with all fried snacks. This sauce can be made and served immediately or placed in a tightly closed jar and refrigerated for use from time to time.

INGREDIENTS

4 hot peppers, scotch bonnet or habanero peppers, coarsely ground
1 medium onion, ground with pepper
½ cup boiled smoked Herring or Bonga flakes
4 tablespoons vegetable oil
¼ teaspoon salt
1 small Maggi cube
1 teaspoon tomato paste
2 tablespoons water

1. Put pepper, onion, fish flakes and oil to a medium pot and bring to a boil over medium heat. Add salt, Maggi, tomato paste, and water and bring to a boil. Taste and add more salt if desired.
2. Continue to simmer until all ingredients are soft and sauce is thick.
3. Remove from heat and set aside until it cools. Spoon into a jar, close tightly, and refrigerate.

Serve with boiled tubers, boiled tree crops, or any fried snack.

Variation: Vegetarian (Hot Pepper Sauce)

INGREDIENTS

2 hot peppers, scotch bonnet or habanero peppers, coarsely ground
1 medium onion, finely chopped
2 cloves garlic, finely chopped
¼ cup vegetable oil of your choice, do not use palm oil
¼ teaspoon salt
1 small Maggi cube
2 tablespoons water

1. Add all the ingredients to a pot and mix together. Bring to a boil over medium heat. Taste and add more salt if desired.
2. Reduce heat to low and simmer until all ingredients are soft.
3. Remove from heat and set aside until it cools.
4. Spoon sauce into a jar. Close the jar tightly and refrigerate.

Serve with boiled tubers, boiled tree crops, or any fried snack.

RICE PAP: This is a very popular snack. It can be eaten as a breakfast meal or simply as a snack. What impresses me about rice pap is its role as a food gift exchanged between religious groups in Sierra Leone. It strikes me as a unifying dish. (See (*Food Story: The Lessons in Tolerance* in this chapter.)

SERVES 4

INGREDIENTS

2 cups brown rice flour (though brown is more ideal, white rice flour can also be used)
2½ cups water
¼ cup sugar (optional)
2 small limes

PREPARATION

1. Pour rice flour into a calabash or large bowl. Sprinkle with a handful of water and mix vigorously until balls start to form. Shake and collect balls from the top. Set balls aside in a separate bowl.
2. Repeat several times, adding a small amount of water each time. Mix, shake, and collect balls until most of the flour is in the form of balls.
3. Dry balls in sun or keep in open tray for 4 to 6 hours to ensure balls are hard. Separate balls by category, from largest to smallest. (Dried balls can be immediately made into rice pap or can be stored in jars for future use.)

COOKING METHOD

1. Pour water into a large pot and bring to a boil over medium heat. Add balls a little at a time - start with largest balls and continue down through to the smallest sizes.
2. As you add balls to the pot, stir slowly and gently with a wooden spoon to prevent balls from sticking together or opening up. Bring pot to a boil over medium heat and continue to cook for 10 minutes or until the balls are cooked right through to the inside. Squeeze a ball between two fingers to confirm.
3. If thick pap is preferred, mix a small amount of leftover flour with water and pour into the pot as you mix gently.
4. Bring to a boil then reduce heat to low and simmer for 5 minutes. Add sugar and mix. Cover and simmer until consistency is as thick as you would like it. Remove pot from heat. Add lime and mix.

Serve as a snack, a breakfast cereal, or the first meal for breaking a fast.

RICE KANYA

SERVES 6

INGREDIENTS

1 cup rice flour
2 cups groundnut paste
1 cup ground sugar (quantity optional)

1. In a large skillet, heat the rice flour over medium heat. Stir continuously for 20 minutes or until flour is slightly brown. Remove from heat and grind while it is still hot.
2. Sieve to remove any hard particles. Add groundnut paste and sugar and then grind a little or until it is evenly mixed.
3. Organize the mixture into shapes, as you would with cookies, or serve as it is.
4. Store the balance in a tight jar and serve when needed. It can keep for several days.

Serve with a glass of fruit drink, water, or any soda.

Variation: Farina/Gari: Farina, often referred to as *gari,* is a flour that is produced from the cassava tuber through the process of grating and frying. *Kanya* can be prepared using the same method as in the *Rice Kanya* recipe.

RICE *AKARA*

SERVES 4

INGREDIENTS

2 cups rice flour
1 tablespoon sugar (quantity optional)
1 teaspoon baking powder
4 ripe bananas, mashed or blended until all lumps disappear
¼ cup water
1½ cups vegetable oil

1. In a large mixing bowl, mix rice flour, sugar, and baking powder. Then add mashed bananas and mix. Add water and mix until mixture is evenly smooth, then, put aside. Add oil to a skillet and heat over medium heat.
2. Scoop mixture with a teaspoon, drop each scoop into oil, and fry in small batches, turning from side to side until light brown on the outside.
3. Remove and put on absorbent paper to drain oil.

Serve by itself or with pepper sauce.

Variations: Other Types of Flour: Prepare this dish using the *Rice Akara* recipe, but replace the rice flour with wheat flour or ordinary self-rising flour. But, be aware that this variation is referred to as *akara* and not flour *akara.*

BOILED GROUNDNUT

SERVES 4

INGREDIENTS

3 cups raw fresh groundnut in shells
Water, to cover groundnut by 1 inch
1 teaspoon salt

1. Wash groundnut several times to remove mud and other particles.
2. Put groundnut into the pot and add water and salt. Bring to a boil over high heat. Stir and remove from heat.
3. Let stand in hot water for 5 minutes and then turn into colander to drain water.

To eat this snack break each pod, remove groundnut, and eat.

ROASTED GROUNDNUT

Groundnuts are a favorite snack in the region, and people sometimes nibble on them as they walk from place to place. Even so, in Sierra Leone, there is a legend that teaches that 'one cannot walk on any road with a mouthful of roasted groundnut eaten with a bite of bread.' It is a reasonable belief that while ambling along, a person will not concentrate and can bump into something or something can bump into them.

Roasted groundnuts are available ready-made in food stores all over the world; you can also find them in the form of peanut butter or as packets of roasted groundnuts. Traditionally, the raw nuts were removed from the shells, added to a pot, placed over fire, and stirred continuously until lightly brown. Then, it was removed from the fire, allowed to cool, and eaten. It was also ground in a mortar to provide a smooth paste.

GROUNDNUT CAKE

SERVES 6

INGREDIENTS

1 cup ground sugar
½ cup water
1 lime, squeezed, to measure 1 tablespoon juice
2 cups roasted groundnut, peeled

1. Dissolve sugar in water and add to a pot. Bring to a boil over high heat. Stir and continue to boil for 5 minutes or until mixture is light brown.
2. Squeeze juice from lime and add to the pot. Stir in the roasted groundnut. Stir for 2 minutes or until ingredients are evenly mixed and sticking together.
3. Put onto cutting board and spread out using a roller pin (or an equivalent utensil).
4. While still hot, divide into small portions and roll out each portion into little squares or triangles, depending on your preference.
5. Store in an air-tight jar to serve from when ready

BENNISEED CAKE

SERVES 4

INGREDIENTS

1 cup ground sugar
½ cup water
2 cups roasted benniseed
1 lime or 1 tablespoon lime juice

1. Dissolve sugar in water and add to a pot. Bring to a boil over medium heat for 5 minutes or until mixture is light brown.
2. Stir in roasted benniseed and lime (or lime juice). Stir for 2 minutes or until ingredients are evenly mixed and sticking together.
3. Put onto cutting board and spread out using a roller pin (or an equivalent utensil).
4. While still hot, divide into small portions and roll out each portion into little squares or triangles, depending on your preference.
5. Serve immediately or store in an air-tight jar and serve when ready.

COCONUT CAKE

SERVES 4

INGREDIENTS

1 large coconut or 2 cups thin, short slices of coconut
1 cup ground sugar
2 cups water

1. Remove coconut from shell. Cut into thin, short slices and put into a large pot or skillet.
2. Add sugar and water and stir together. Place over medium heat and bring to a boil.
3. Continue to boil and stir until water evaporates and ingredients are sticking together.
4. Put onto cutting board and spread out using a roller pin (or an equivalent utensil).
5. While still hot, divide into small portions and roll out each portion into little squares.

Serve immediately or store in a jar to serve when ready.

FISH BALLS

SERVES 4

INGREDIENTS

2 medium-size fresh whole fish or 8 serving pieces of
    fish fillet, snapper, or tilapia
1 lime
Salt, to taste
1 teaspoon white pepper
¼ cup mashed potato or yam, cooked
2 eggs, broken and mixed
¼ cup flour
1 cup cooking oil for frying

Fish balls with pepper sauce

1. Clean fish and wash thoroughly. Squeeze juice from lime and pour over fish. Season with salt and white pepper. Put fish into a pot and simmer over low heat until water evaporates and fish is dry.
2. Remove from heat and allow fish to cool. Separate flesh from bones and discard bones. With a wooden spoon or your hand, break up the fish into tiny pieces. Add mashed potato (or yam) and mix together until all the ingredients blend evenly. Fold the mixture into little balls, drop each into egg mixture, and roll over in the flour.
3. In a skillet, heat oil over medium heat and fry balls, turning from side to side until brown.

CRAB BALLS

SERVES 4

INGREDIENTS

2 cups crabmeat, steamed
1 lime
1 teaspoon white pepper
Salt, to taste
¼ cup mashed potato or yam, cooked
2 eggs, broken and mixed
¼ cup flour
1 cup cooking oil for frying

1. Put crabmeat in a bowl. Squeeze juice from lime and pour over crabmeat. Season with salt and white pepper.
2. Combine steamed crabmeat with mashed potato (or yam) and with a wooden spoon, mix together until all the ingredients blend evenly. Fold the mixture into little balls, drop each into egg mixture, and roll over in the flour.
3. In a skillet, heat oil over medium heat and fry balls, turning from side to side until brown.

HERRING: You can fry whole herring or the fillet. See recipes below for Fried Herring and In Batter (Herring Bites). Remember never to add salt because it will make it extremely salty; the other seasonings, listed in the recipes, will do the trick.

FRIED HERRING BITES

SERVES 4

INGREDIENTS

8 whole fresh herring
1 lime
2 cloves garlic, ground
½ teaspoon white pepper
1 Maggi cube, broken into powder

1. Clean herring, taking off scales and cleaning the inside. Remove head and discard.
2. Cut a ring around the point where the tail joins the trunk of the fish. Squeeze fish gently on the sides. This will detach flesh from the bone.
3. With two fingers of each hand, hold the fish tight at the point of the ring. Draw the fish, with the fingers facing the body of the fish, and pull towards the head while holding firmly on the tail end. This will remove the central bone structure of the fish.
4. Rinse the fish and cut into serving sizes. Squeeze juice from lime and pour over fish.
5. Mix in garlic, white pepper, and Maggi. Marinate for ½ hour.
6. In a skillet, heat oil over medium heat and fry fish, turning from side to side until golden brown.

Serve with hot pepper sauce.

Alternatively, you can clean the herring and leave it whole. Season as in the recipe for *Fried Herring Bites* and follow the same cooking procedure.

Herring can also be prepared as soup for a main meal. See the *Main Dishes: Stews and Spicy Fish* chapter for recipe.

Variation: In Batter (Herring Bites)

INGREDIENTS

8 whole fresh herring
1 lime
2 cloves garlic, ground
½ teaspoon white pepper
1 Maggi cube, broken into powder
1 cup flour, spread out on a plate
2 eggs, broken and mixed, set aside in a bowl

1. Clean herring, taking off scales and cleaning the inside. Remove head and discard.
2. Cut a ring around the point where the tail joins the trunk of the fish. Squeeze fish gently on the sides. This will detach flesh from the bone.
3. With two fingers of each hand, hold the fish tight at the point of the ring. Draw the fish, with the fingers facing the body of the fish, and pull towards the head while holding firmly on the tail end. This will remove the central bone structure of the fish.
4. Rinse the fish and cut into serving sizes. Squeeze juice from lime and pour over fish. Mix in garlic, white pepper, and Maggi. Marinate for ½ hour.
5. Drop each piece of into the egg mixture so that the piece is evenly soaked with the egg mixture. Repeat with each piece.
6. Roll each fish now coated with egg mixture over in the flour so that the fish is evenly coated with the flour.
7. In a skillet, heat oil over medium heat and fry fish, turning from side to side until golden brown.

ROAST BEEF ON SKEWERS

SERVES 10 to 15

INGREDIENTS

3 pound boneless beef, chopped into serving cubes
1 lime
Salt, to taste
2 cloves garlic, pressed or ground
1 Maggi cube, broken into powder
1 ginger, ground
1 Pepper, ground, or 1 teaspoon ground paprika, (optional)
1 large onion, chopped into large squire slices
1 tablespoon groundnut paste
1 tablespoon cooking oil
1 teaspoon tomato paste
15 skewers

1. Cut beef into bite-size pieces, wash, and drain off water. Squeeze juice from lime and pour over meat.
2. Season with salt, garlic, Maggi, ginger, and pepper. Add large onion slices.
3. Mix groundnut paste with oil and tomato paste until it becomes liquid. Stir in the meat and generously rub mixture all over the beef.
4. Cover and marinate in a refrigerator for 1 hour or longer. Thread beef and onion slices onto skewers.
5. Place the beef on skewers in a tray, cover with aluminum foil and continue to refrigerate.
6. Meanwhile, organize a charcoal fire for direct grilling. When all the charcoal is lighted up and fire is very hot, remove beef from the refrigerator and grill over fire for 5 minutes.

BEANS *AKARA* AND *OLELEH*: Beans *Akara* and *Oleleh* are eaten throughout the region. They are healthy and tasty and can be eaten as snacks, appetizers, or interesting side dishes for main meals. They are also popular dishes for lunch and breakfast. In Sierra Leone, it is common for mothers to fill a loaf of bread with Beans *Akara*, which acts as a sandwich-like treat that children can take to school as lunch. It is a very easy meal to make.

As advised in the *Planning and Preparing Ahead* chapter, you can always clean the beans in advance of cooking. I usually do, and in this way, I can always make my Beans *Akara* or *Oleleh* as quickly as needed.

Cooking methods for both dishes are different. While Beans *Akara* is cooked using the frying method, *Oleleh* is cooked using the steaming method. To steam *Oleleh*, you will need a steamer. If you do not have a steamer, use any pot but insert a stainless metal frame inside the pot to serve as a steaming rack. You can also line the bottom of any pot with aluminum foil making sure it is above the water level so that it can serve as a bed separating the water from the beans mixture.

BEANS *AKARA*

SERVES 6

INGREDIENTS

2 cups black-eyed beans, cleaned (see the *Planning and Preparing Ahead* chapter)
½ teaspoon salt
1 pepper (optional)
1 small onion, finely chopped
¼ cups cold water
1 cup vegetable oil for deep-frying

Beans Akara. From left, black eyed beans unclean, cleaned beans, ground beans ready for frying and end product...beans Akara at the bottom.

1. Turn clean beans into a blender and blend for 3 seconds. Add salt, pepper, onion, and water. Blend into smooth paste.
2. Turn paste into a large bowl. Beat with a wooden spoon or by hand to get rid of any air in the mixture. Beat until smooth and creamy, like mashed potatoes, and easily clings to the spoon and gently falls from it.
3. In a skillet, heat oil over medium heat. With a teaspoon, scoop mixture and drop, one at a time, into the oil and fry in small batches, turning from side to side until evenly golden brown.
4. Remove from oil and put on absorbent paper to drain oil.

Serve with a glass of water or fruit drink.

OLELEH/MOIN-MOIN

SERVES 6

INGREDIENTS

2 cups black-eyed beans, soaked and
    cleaned (see the *Planning and
    Preparing Ahead* chapter)
1 hot pepper (optional)
1 medium onion
¼ cup plus ½ cups warm water
2 tablespoons palm oil or other
    vegetable oil
1 small Maggi cube
½ teaspoon salt or to taste
½ cup large steamed fresh fish
    flakes, corn beef, or a few slices
   boiled eggs (optional, do not add if preparing vegetarian meal)
Custard cups, banana leaves, or aluminum foil

Oleleh made with fish

1. Put clean beans into a blender and blend for 3 seconds. Add pepper, onion, ¼ cup water, and blend until smooth. Add the remaining water, oil, Maggi, and salt. Then blend for 3 seconds. Put mixture into a bowl. Ensure that there are no bones in the fish flakes. Add the fish flakes (or a substitute).

2. If using banana leaves, clean leaves with water, then hold leaves directly over low heat for 1 minute. This will soften the leaves. Organize leaves into pouches so that each can hold some beans mixture without causing any leakages. If using aluminum foil organize them as well into pouches. If using custard tins, line them with oil. Put these aside.

3. Spoon 3 tablespoons beans mixture into the banana leaves or aluminum foil pouches or fill custard cups to about ¾ into the custard cups. Wrap leaves or aluminum foil tightly or cover the custard cups using a cellophane paper. This is to ensure that water does not get into the mixture while it is steaming.

4. Place into steamer or pot lined with a steaming rack or aluminum foil. Cook undisturbed over high heat for 50 minutes to 1 hour or until the beans mixture is firm. Remove from cup (or banana leaves or aluminum foil) and serve hot.

Serve hot as a snack or appetizer.

Variations: OTHER OILS (OLELEH/MOIN-MOIN) Cook this dish following the cooking procedure for *Oleleh/Moin-Moin* but omit the fish or meat. Although *Oleleh* tastes great when cooked with palm oil, it also tastes wonderfully yummy when cooked with any of the other vegetable cooking oils - such as groundnut oil. If this is preferred, do not hesitate to use instead of palm oil.

Also note that if preparing a vegetable meal, you can omit all the fish and meat and just cook the beans

FRIED SNACKS: Fried snacks are a common sight on the streets of West African countries. Vendors carry them in small packets to sell. They are also prepared in homes and eaten as snacks at any time during the day. Some of these fried snacks can be served with side vegetables, like cucumbers, green salad, tomatoes, or even a salad of one's choice.

FRIED RIPE PLANTAIN

SERVES 3

INGREDIENTS

2 large plantains, half ripe with yellow skin
Salt, to taste
2 cups vegetable oil

1. Cut each plantain into 3 pieces and peel off skin. Slice plantain into 1-inch slices - lengthwise or round. Sprinkle a little bit of salt all over and mix gently with your hand to ensure plantain slices are evenly salted.
2. In a skillet, heat oil over medium heat. (Use a deep fryer, if possible.) Place plantain slices side by side and not on top of each other. Fry slowly in small batches, turning from side to side to prevent burning.
3. Remove each slice of plantain as it turns golden brown. Put onto plate lined with absorbent paper to absorb the oil.

Serve as a snack or appetizer, a side dish with *joloff* rice, or as a main meal accompanied by stew, black-eyed beans sauce, fried fish, and a bowl of garden salad.

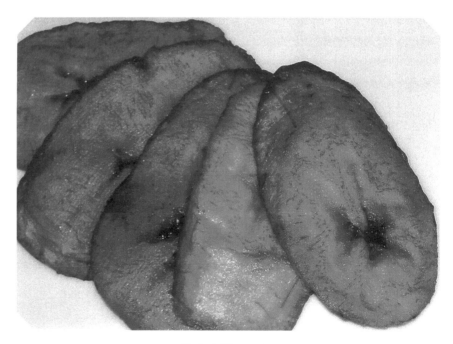

Fried Plantains

FRIED GREEN PLANTAIN

SERVES 4

INGREDIENTS

3 plantains, unripe
1 cup water
1 tablespoon salt
1 cup vegetable oil

1. Peel plantain, rinse, and slice into thin, long or round shape. Add salt to water and soak sliced plantain for 10 minutes. Drain and leave in colander to dry.
2. In a skillet, heat oil over medium heat and deep-fry. Turn onto plate lined with absorbent paper to absorb the oil.

Serve as a snack or appetizer.

FRIED GREEN BANANA: Green bananas can be fried using the same procedure used for *Fried Ripe Plantains*.

FRIED SWEET POTATO

SERVES 4

INGREDIENTS

6 medium sweet potatoes
Salt, to taste
3 cups vegetable oil

1. Peel potatoes and wash in a bowl of cold water. Slice lengthwise into ½-inch pieces. Rinse, remove from water, and then season with salt.
2. In a skillet, heat oil over medium heat and deep-fry. Turn onto plate lined with absorbent paper to absorb the oil.

Serve as a snack or appetizer.

FRIED BREADFRUIT

SERVES 6

INGREDIENTS

1 large breadfruit
Salt, to taste

1. Peel breadfruit and slice lengthwise into ½-inch pieces. Season with salt.
2. In a skillet, heat oil over medium heat and deep-fry.
3. Turn onto plate lined with absorbent paper to absorb the oil.

Serve as a snack or appetizer.

ROASTED/GRILLED TUBERS AND TREE CROPS: Breadfruit, sweet potatoes, and plantains can serve as delicious snacks when roasted or grilled.

ROASTED BREADFRUIT

SERVES 4

INGREDIENT

1 medium breadfruit

1. Light the charcoal fire or heat the broiler.
2. Place the breadfruit over the fire and roast for 30 to 45 minutes, turning from side to side.
3. Press with thumb or put a tooth pick through to test breadfruit's readiness. Breadfruit is ready when it is soft (roasting time will depend on size and level of fire).
4. Remove from fire and peel off the black skin, cut into serving cubes, and serve.

Serve alone, with salt and palm oil, or with pepper sauce.

ROASTED SWEET POTATOE: Prepare using the cooking procedure in the *Roasted Breadfruit* recipe. This will roast in 20 to 25 minutes, depending on the size and level of fire.

ROASTED PLANTAIN: For this recipe, use the plantain that is just about to ripen. Peel the whole plantain. Prepare using the cooking procedure for *Roasted Breadfruit*.

ROASTED CASSAVA TUBER: Prepare using cooking procedure for *Roasted Breadfruit*. Cassava can also be roasted peeled or unpeeled.

Food Story: The Lessons in Tolerance

Rice Pap is a snack that many people eat as a morning cereal. During the Muslim fast month of Ramadan, it is a favorite first meal after a day of fasting. In Sierra Leone, where Muslims and Christians live side by side in harmony, many Christians often prepare rice pap and send it to their Muslim neighbors during Ramadan. Many Muslims do the same for the Christians during the Easter period. Because many Muslims are aware that Christ fasted for 40 days and 40 nights, they do this with the belief that their Christian neighbors also fast during this period.

This practice always reminds me that one of the most remarkable things about Sierra Leone is its religious tolerance, a fact that many people do not seem to know. In Sierra Leone, we have Catholic priests and bishops who have parents or other close relatives who are strong Muslims. We also have had a president who is a devoted Muslim, but whose wife was a devoted Catholic. It is a country where interreligious activities are encouraged. The "Radio Maria," a Catholic Radio Network located in Makeni, Sierra Leone, encourages Christians and Muslims to dialogue with one another.

Looking back at my youth gives me a good insight into the roots of religious tolerance in my country. It reminds me that it truly is about what children see and feel when they are growing up. As a child, I attended Catholic schools, and when I wanted to become a Catholic, my Muslim mother encouraged and supported me. She was happy for me, and she told me that it was important to worship according to my own beliefs. My mother made it clear to me that Muslims and Christians worship the same God and there were very few differences between the two groups, including the methods of worshiping. I still remember the broad, beautiful smile on her face the day she presented me with a white dress to wear for my baptismal ceremony. My mother and I respected each other's religions and supported one another whenever possible.

During the holidays, she used to encourage me to take my Bible to my uncle, Allieu, so that we could talk about our two religions. My uncle was highly respected for his vast knowledge about the Quran and I was very knowledgeable about the Bible. I was able to read the Bible in Mende, my first language, and so I was able to read the passages, as they were written, to my Uncle, who could not speak or read English. Thus, our readings were always very interesting because we exchanged views about certain areas of our two books.

I now believe that this same type of dialogue must have been going on in other households throughout the country. The people of Sierra Leone saw the good fruit of this during the years our country was at war. Though several people tried to use religion to intensify the conflict, they all failed.

Fruits: Fresh Fruits

Many tropical fruits grow in West Africa, including mangoes, oranges, pineapples, pawpaws, ripe bananas, and grapefruit. Many of the fruits in the wild are still waiting to be domesticated. Fruits are eaten as snacks and as desserts after meals. To eat, simply peel and serve.

Some tropical fruits. From left, basket of mangoes and oranges; with bananas and pawpaw in the background.

Beverages

Drinks   Ginger Beer
Variation: Flavored Ginger
Sorrel
Lime
Lemongrass
Other Fruits
Palm Wine and Fresh *Cacao*

Food Story   A Fruity Beverage Story

BEVERAGES

GINGER BEER

SERVES 10 to 15

INGREDIENTS

15 cups water
2 cups ginger, peeled, grated, or ground
2 cups ground sugar (optional)
1 cup cloves

1. Put water and ginger into a pot and bring to a boil over high heat.
2. Remove from heat and let stand until sediments settle at the bottom. Allow the drink to cool.
3. Drain in sieve to remove sediments and then add sugar and cloves. Using a wooden spoon, stir vigorously and taste.
4. Turn into serving jars and refrigerate to chill.

Serve alone in a glass or with ice.

FLAVORED GINGER

Prepare using the *Ginger Beer* recipe. But, after adding sugar and cloves, add 3 cups of your preferred drink. Mix vigorously and taste. Turn into jars and refrigerate.

SORREL: Drinks made from dried Sorrel flowers known as *jus de bissap* in Senegal, *zobo* in Nigeria, and sorrel in many other countries.

SORREL

SERVES 8 to 10

INGREDIENTS

5 cups sorrel dried flowers, washed and rinsed in cold water
10 cups water
3 cups sugar or to taste
½ cup cloves

1. Put sorrel flowers and water into a pot and bring to a boil over high heat. Remove immediately from heat and let stand until sediments settle at the bottom.
2. Allow drink to cool. Drain in sieve to remove sediments. Add sugar and cloves. Using a wooden spoon stir vigorously and taste.
3. Turn into serving jars and refrigerate to chill.

Serve cool alone or with ice.

LIME

SERVES 2

INGREDIENTS

2 cups water
10 fresh limes, squeezed to extract juice
¼ cup sugar (optional)

1. Bring water to a boil over medium heat. Add juice from lime and sugar. Using a wooden spoon, stir well.
2. Remove from heat and allow drink to cool..
3. Turn into jar and refrigerate to chill.

Serve alone or with ice cubes.

Alternatively, you can add sugar to any quantity of freshly squeezed lime juice and keep in the freezer. When ready to drink, just defrost, add sugar, and boiled water. Allow to cool and then turn into a jar.

LEMONGRASS

SERVES 2

INGREDIENTS

1 handful of fresh lemongrass
3 cups water
Sugar to taste (optional)

1. Wash lemongrass several times in cold water until very clean and then put into a pot.
2. Add water. Cover and bring to a boil over high heat. Continue to cook for 15 minutes.
3. Remove from heat and drain the liquid from lemongrass.
4. Pour liquid into a teapot and serve with sugar.

OTHER FRUITS: A variety of fruits can be squeezed and their liquid used as drinks.

PALM WINE AND FRESH *CACAO*: Both fresh palm wine and cacao drinks are naturally produced using traditional preparation methods.

The production of palm wine is a simple process because it comes directly from the sap of the palm tree. Someone climbs a palm tree or a raffia palm, makes a hole in the trunk at the neck of the palm, and then ties a container around the trunk and leaves it for a day or two. The liquid sap, which in effect is the fresh palm wine, starts collecting in the container in small drops. (In Sierra Leone, the fresh palm wine is referred to as "a drink from God to man." This is because the drink simply drops from the hole in the trunk of a tall palm tree and is collected and consumed. Furthermore, it tastes so fresh; it feels like a drink handed down by a most kind and powerful God.)

After two days, the owner returns to the palm tree and collects the fresh palm wine. He returns to his village and shares with his family, friends, and neighbors, usually making him a very popular man. Some people, however, make a living by palm wine tapping and sell their product in small palm wine huts.

Fresh *cacao* drink comes from cocoa beans when they are being fermented in readiness for drying. Though this drink is available and very popular in West Africa, it is not readily available in large quantities; because of its production method, only very small quantities can be produced.

Food Story: A Fruity Beverage Story

I remember the 1960's in my village. Life was peaceful; people did the things they could do with love and affection. In addition to subsistence-level crops, like rice, one major cash crop grown by each family was cocoa, also known as cacao. Fruit, such as mangoes, pawpaws, and oranges, were also abundant. We ate fruit at anytime of the day; for the children, just picking the fresh fruit and eating them was fun. The thought of those delicious fruit – the golden, yellow flesh of the pawpaws, the sweet taste of the oranges and mangoes – always delighted us. The recollection of the *cacao* harvest still brings back fond memories of my village – a village that was unfortunately destroyed during the country's ten-year war.

Cacao was harvested after the harvesting of rice, which was the staple food among my people And, there were other types of food, like tubers and tree crops, which were also in abundance. We, the children, had a lot to eat, and we enjoyed doing our chores and listening to folk stories during twilight. Watching the football-shaped, ripe, greenish-yellow *cacao* pods that hung from the cocoa tree was a good pastime for us. We would occasionally chew on the dried cocoa beans. Looking back, I can still feel the air of happiness that engulfed all of us during *cacao* harvesting and processing. I can still remember the fruity smell of the drink that was extracted from the cocoa beans; a drink that was considered medicinal and believed to regulate the stomach. It is as if I am transported back to the village of my childhood.

Though the juicy, wine-like drink, extracted from the cocoa beans during fermentation, created a sense of celebration for children, the adults looked forward to the cash they made from the beans. The popular, finished products, in the form of powdered cocoa, sat dusted in a Lebanese owner's shop consumed only by his family members and the few occasional buyers who recognized and could afford it. These buyers were mainly teachers who taught at the village's only elementary school and a few others who worked for the railway. The rest of us did not know what chocolates were. Most of us were content with drinking the fermented liquid and chewing the dried beans. We missed out on nothing.

Today, looking at the same *cacao* tree reminds me of those happy times. But, it is tinged with a mixture of sadness because I know now what I did not know then. Unlike Sierra Leone, where *cacao* is produced on small family holdings, other developing countries that produce *cacao* on a large scale force children to work on these farms. And, those who do the hard work, the producers and the laborers, get very little for their labor. I now understand the injustice that surrounds the crop.

The good news is that the world is now looking at this injustice and trying to correct the mistake. When this error is finally corrected, I know I will again look at this crop with the same happy feeling that I had as a child; a feeling of happiness that comes from the thought of my dear old *cacao* plant and its pods.

Glossary

Akara	Bite-size, deep-fried fritters made out of different types of batter with main ingredients like ground black-eyed beans, rice flour, and other types of flour
Beans *Akara*	A dish made solely from peeled, ground black-eyed beans formed into balls and deep-fried
Benniseed	Small, oval seeds also known as sesame seed
Bitter Leaf	Small, evergreen vegetable leaf
Bonga	Type of small and tasty fish, usually smoked and cooked with some dishes
Bor-boueh	A special type of wild mango seed. Cooked as a vegetable, after drying and grinding
Breadfruit	A large, seedless fruit used as a carbohydrate meal in the region
Bush Meat	Meat from some edible wild animals, such as deer
Bush Okra	Dark green, slippery vegetable also known by different names, such as *crain-crain*
Cassava	From a woody shrub whose tuberous root (cassava tuber) is a major source of carbohydrates. Its green leaves have a high concentration of vitamins, proteins, and minerals, which include high levels of fiber and potassium. In some parts of the world cassava is also called *yuca* or *manioc*.
Cacao Drink	Wine-like drink produced when the cocoa bean (also known as *cacao*) goes through the fermenting process
Crain-Crain	The name in Sierra Leone for bush okra
Cutting Grass	A very tasty bush meat considered a delicacy in the West African region. It is believed to be very high in protein and very low in fat.
Domba	Type of *fufu* made from boiled, starchy tubers, like cassava
Egusi	A type of melon seed, used as thickener in soups and some sauces

Farina	A form of textured flour made from grated and roasted cassava. Also known as *gari*
Fasei	Type of crayfish. When dried and ground, used as a condiment in cooking mixed sauces
Fufu	Staple food made from fermented tubers, like cassava
Garden Egg	A bud-like vegetable with high fiber content
Gari	Same as *farina*
Gbuhing	Vegetable also known as fiddlehead in the West
Ginger Beer	Non-alcoholic drink made from ginger
Groundnut	Also known as peanut
Jew's Mellow	Vegetable (see bush okra)
Joloff Rice	Well-loved rice dish cooked by combining rice and many other ingredients
Jolabetei	Another name for Potato Leaf Sauce
Jute Leaf	Vegetable also known as *crain-crain*, bush okra, etc. (see bush okra)
Kanya	Candy-like snack made from rice flour and other ingredients
Kenda	A condiment made from the fermented seeds of a special tree plant
Kontomire	Cocoyam Leaf Stew made in Ghana
Kola Nut	A seed kernel of a large African tree used during social ceremonies
Kormaphai	A type of dried mushroom that grows in Sierra Leone
Kporway	A type of mushroom that grows wild in Sierra Leone. It is like a portobello mushroom, in appearance and taste.
Lubi	Produced locally from local materials. Used as bicarbonate of soda.
Maggi	A trade name for a seasoning that is very common in West Africa. In the absence of Maggi, you can use other seasoning cubes for soups and stews.
Mixed sauce	Dish made when proteins, vegetables, and other ingredients are cooked together

Muranda	Another name for *crain-crain* (see bush okra)
Molokhia	Another name for *crain-crain* (see muranda)
Ogbornor	Nigerian name for *Bor-boueh*
Ogiri	Condiment made from fermented *benniseed*
Oleleh	Pie-like dish made from ground black-eyed beans
Palaver Sauce	Same as mixed sauce
Palm Kernel	Nut from the palm fruit
Palm Oil	Oil extracted from the palm fruit
Palm Wine	Wine from the palm tree
Partee	Dish made from a blend of different types of tubers and other ingredients
Paw-Paw-Daah	Special herb used for cooking sea fish, freshwater fish, and shellfish dishes
Pemahuin	Rice dish cooked with a blend of potato leaves and other ingredients steamed over the cooking rice
Pillaah	Type of green, leafy vegetable
Sakii Tomboi	Sierra Leonean name for Cassava Leaf Sauce
Tola	Seed from a special type of wild mango tree. When the seed is dried, ground, and cooked with other ingredients, the end result is a nice mixed sauce called *Tola* Sauce.
Torworgbortoh:	Sierra Leonean name for Broad Beans Sauce

Author Rachel Massaquoi